NATIVE AMERICAN HISTORY *of* SAVANNAH

NATIVE AMERICAN HISTORY
of
SAVANNAH

MICHAEL FREEMAN

THE History PRESS

Published by The History Press
Charleston, SC
www.historypress.com

Front cover: Yamacraw Village. Copyright Charlie Swerdlow, historydepicted.com.

First published 2018

Manufactured in the United States

ISBN 9781467138314

Library of Congress Control Number: 2018932122

CONTENTS

Preface 7
Acknowledgements 11
Introduction 13

1. The Beginnings 17
2. Guales on a Mission 24
3. The Mississippian Culture Was a Big Deal 28
4. The Yamasee War Was the Creek Vietnam War 40
5. The Creeks Keep Their Home Fires Burning 45
6. Tomochichi, a Founder of Georgia 52
7. Toonahowi, Forever Young 66
8. Malatchi, Born to Rule 73
9. Senauki, the Good Mother 78
10. Mary Musgrove, the Woman Who Ran with the Wolves 83
11. The Muskogees, Gone but not Forgotten 104
12. The Legacy of the Native Americans of Savannah 110

Bibliography 121
Index 125
About the Author 128

PREFACE

In 1996, the Olympic yachting competition was held in Savannah. Sailors from all over the world stayed in the Olympic Village in the new Marriott Hotel at the end of Savannah's River Walk. On the rear balcony overlooking the Savannah River stands a monument to Hernando de Soto. It is, in some ways, a confusing monument. It was placed there by a local university's Spanish Club and the Catholic diocese, among others. It is presented as recognition and an apology to the Native Americans for their treatment and removal from this land. The following is a quote from the plaque: "Acknowledging error and truth we dedicate this monument to an era of diverse religious and social consciousness in our history hoping to generate a new faith in the renewed quest for universal justice and peace among people of all races and creeds."

It is a belated recognition of the tragic injustice committed by early explorers and colonists of Georgia. The monument was obviously placed there in preparation for the Olympic yachting games Savannah hosted in 1996. It does represent the spirit of the Olympics.

But to my thinking, it also shows our ambiguous thoughts about the legacy of the Native Americans. It appears to be a large bust in honor of the exploitive explorer Hernando de Soto. Unless you read one of three dedication plaques, you cannot reach any other conclusion. No Indian presence is found anywhere on the monument. The Native Americans have been removed from the story. The Savannah story is a story about how we lived and not how the Indians lived or who they are. In this book, I attempt

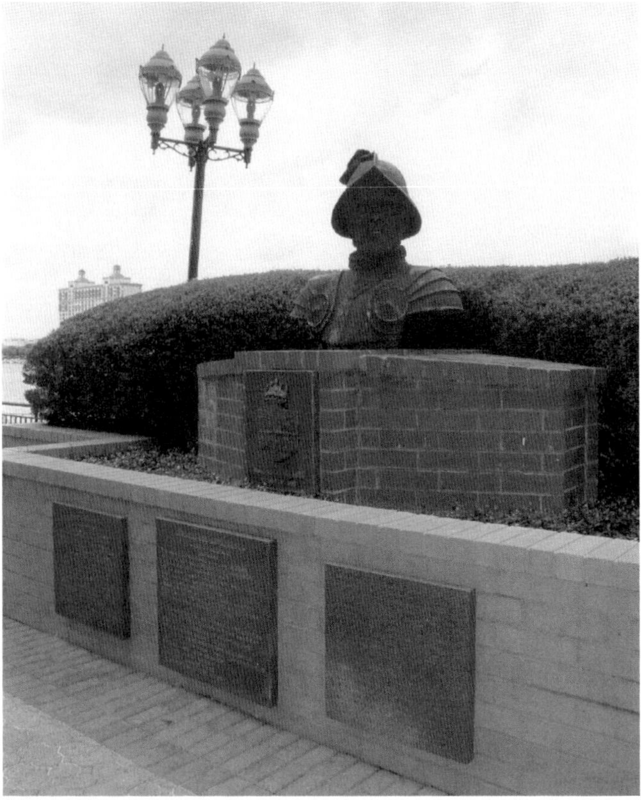

Right: De Soto monument. *Author's collection.*

Below: Plaque on De Soto monument. *Author's collection.*

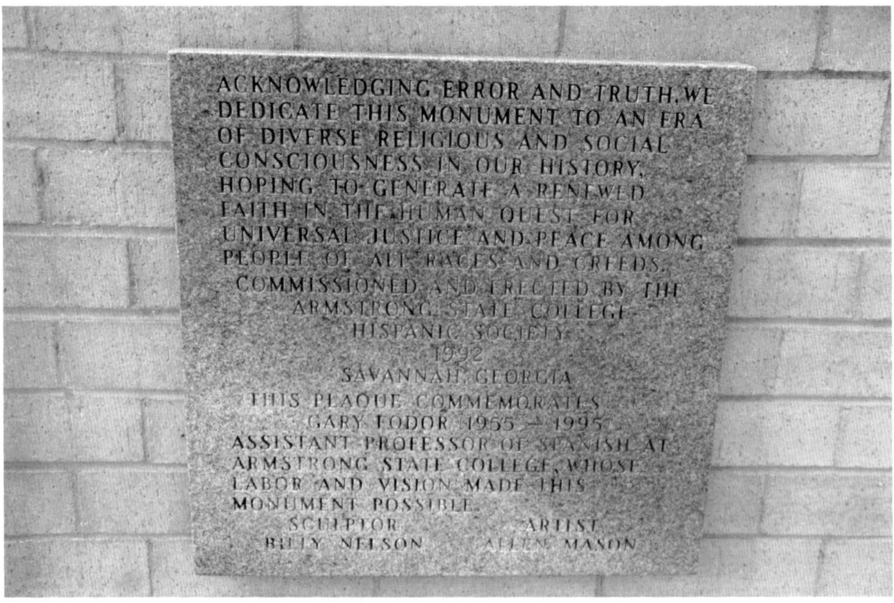

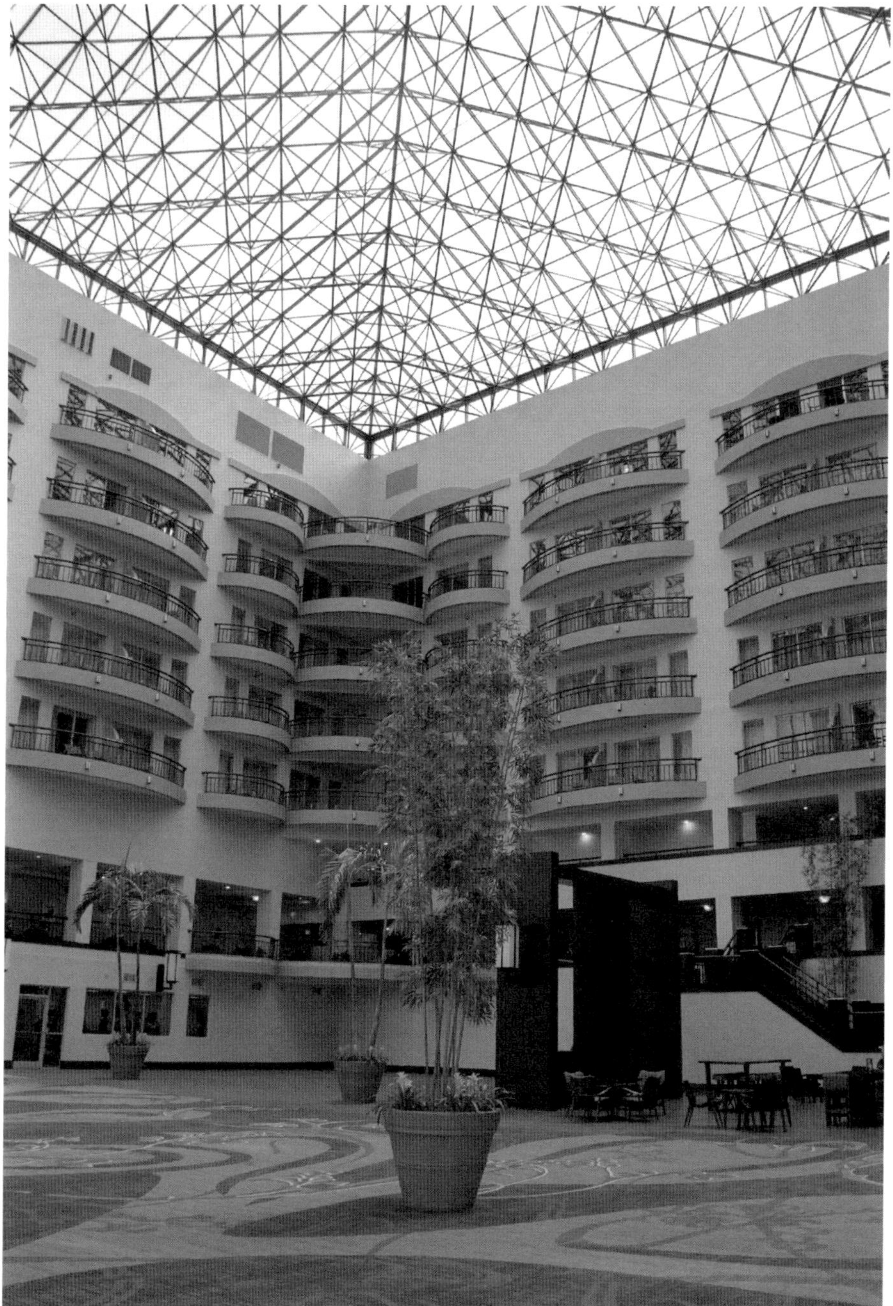

The 1996 Olympic Yachting Village in Savannah. *Author's collection.*

to tell the stories of Savannah's Native Americans. It is my hope this will in part bring back the presence of Tomochichi, Mary Musgrove and other Native Americans as a force that helped propel the City of Savannah and the State of Georgia forward.

ACKNOWLEDGEMENTS

As a rule, books are never completed without a lot of help from your friends. I am extremely appreciative of two friends who lent me a hand as advisors, editors and counselors, Karen and Sha. I want to thank Ira and Helen for allowing me time at their beautiful home in the mountains to write. To my wife, Chris, I owe thanks for patience, editing, counsel and many other things. I also need to thank my children, Philip, Maya and Dorothy, for their continuous love. Finally, I want to thank my editor at The History Press, Amanda Irle, for above and beyond assistance. So, to all of you, one more time, thanks for helping to make this book a reality.

INTRODUCTION

The heritage of Savannah's Native Americans is old and glorious. To fully understand this heritage, we must return to the beginnings of the populating of the Americas. Their heritage spans (16,500 BCE to present day) from one of the giants of civilization, the Meso-Americans, to the eastward expansion of these people. The eastward expansion included the great Mississippian culture; the Mississippian Indians eventually met the predecessors of the Woodland and Paleolithic Indians. These Native Americans would form the Creek Confederation, including some Guale and Cherokee Indians. Finally, a small exiled tribe from the confederation called the Yamacraws formed on a bluff where Savannah is now located.

The British, likewise, trace their heritage through the Greeks, Romans, Saxons and Vikings to proclaim their proud culture. Lord James Oglethorpe and Mico Tomochichi were the quintessential personages of their two cultures. Their meeting forever changed this land we call Georgia.

These two cultures, each with a complex and proud heritage, confronted each other with the advent of the British settling of Georgia. These two cultures that thought they understood each other did not. The British considered themselves the bringers of civilization and thus a better way of being in the world. The Native Americans were troubled by the British acquisitive nature and belief in holding land as private property. The Native Americans had an openness to learning from others and the world about them. They did not view truth as solely their own but could find truth in others. This was unlike the British, who felt called to civilize the world and make it their own. Thus, the natives thought the British were people from whom they could learn. The British considered the Native Americans in need of civilizing.

The British saw the Native Americans as an economic resource at best and, at worst, in need of cultural and personal salvation. The Europeans, for their part, did bring the Indians much desired domesticated animals. But with the animals came diseases that had been brewed in the warmer climes of Europe's cities. The Europeans had long since built immunities to these diseases, but the Native Americans had not. The cloths and furs of animals spread the viruses even further, seriously depleting the Indian population. The Europeans did not know what they wrought, but their good intentions and economic trade with the Indians made the Native Americans vulnerable to epidemics from the European continent.

The Native Americans, for their part, sought trade with the Europeans, for the newcomers had wondrous products that made hunting and domestic life easier. So they strengthened and sustained the Europeans in the early days until the Europeans learned to survive in this country by themselves. As long as they were trading partners, the two sides could reap mutual benefits and live in relative peace. The Native Americans saw trade as a covenant between two people to look after the welfare of each other. The British saw trade strictly as a business transaction with no obligations. When the British became comfortable in what they interpreted as their new land, trouble brewed. The British wanted to put the land to "good" use, while the Native Americans saw wilderness preserves for hunting, gathering and villages with a shared garden. The British saw wasted, unused land to be settled within the wilderness. Where the Indians saw land as communal, the British saw an endless sea of settlers coming from the poorhouses, debtors' prisons and streets starting their lives anew in America with their own private property. This would be the constant conflict. The Native Americans had a reduced population and the Europeans had endless poor people in search of land to call their own and seeking to better their status in life.

The Europeans called Georgia the debatable lands—land that was contested between three European powers: the British expanding from the north, the French expanding from the west and the Spanish expanding up from the south. The Native Americans, who had lived there for centuries, were caught in between these three powers negotiating territory that had been their shared homeland. Outnumbered and outgunned, the Native Americans negotiated for their survival by playing one European country against the other until the British became the dominant power. The advent of British power brought the loss of a significant bargaining chip for the Indians. Now the real possibility of the Indians being ousted from the land—as the French and Spanish had been—became an inevitable predicament. They had to learn to deal with the British politically or go to war; a quick reality check would confirm that any war with the British was very unlikely to end in favor of the Native Americans. Meanwhile, as time passed, the colonists began to call themselves natives, or owners of this land. As this philosophy spread throughout the colonies, the colonists became less inclined to consider the Native Americans as partners but as economic and imperialistic hindrances. This is the conundrum in which the Native Americans of Savannah found themselves when the good ship *Anne* brought the first settlers from England.

1

THE BEGINNINGS

The first people to inhabit the North American West were big animal hunters who were chasing mastodons, giant sloths, giant beavers, *Glyptodon*—a large, armored mammal and relative of the armadillo—saber-toothed tigers and other animals, called megafauna. The hunt for these animals led them to cross the Bering Strait. Because of the severe cold weather, the strait had created a land and ice bridge that gave early peoples access to North America. This bridge existed between 45,000 and 12,000 BCE. It is believed these hunters crossed this bridge about 17,000 years ago. The megafauna preceded their crossing by 5,000 years and were well established in North America before the hunters followed. This theory, though rather old, continues to comply with new discoveries made about what the scientists call the first people to inhabit North America: the Paleo-Indians.

A newer theory posits the peopling of eastern North America by Europeans at about the same time of the Bering Strait crossing. Early Europeans made their way west because of the scarcity of food in Europe during the Ice Age. They crossed over in the Nova Scotia area and entered in the northeastern United States. This group journeyed south, not west, because the Appalachian Mountains made travel southward the easier trek. Eventually, the two groups, one from Asia and the other from Europe, spread out, ultimately melding their different cultures. This caused a hybridization of cultures and unique, new civilizations.

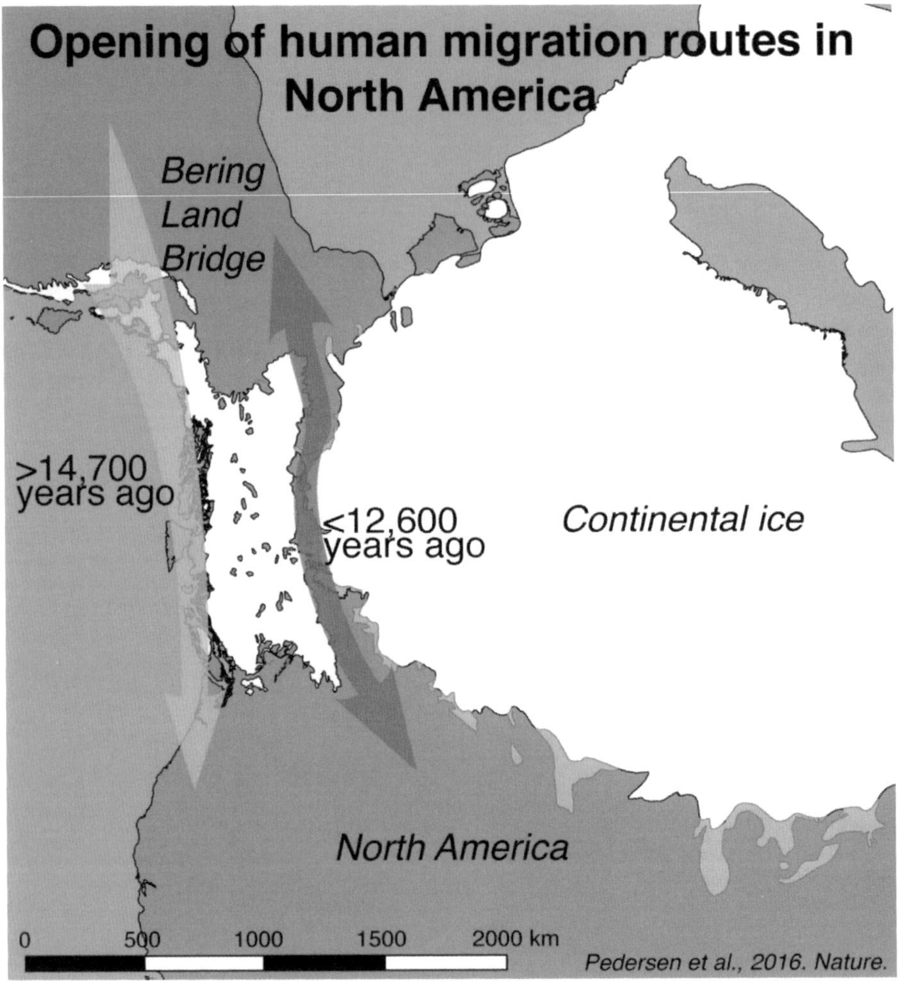

Map of Bering Strait. *Mikkel Winther Pedersen, Natural History Museum of Denmark.*

But let us not get too far ahead of the story. The Paleo-Indians were the first people who crossed the Bering Sea. They usually traveled in groups of between twenty and sixty. They migrated with the animals that they hunted for food. They used primitive stone tools to accomplish their daily tasks, such as hunting, cooking, camping and other rudimentary chores of a nomadic people. These early Indians followed big game for weeks at a time for a kill and then feasted for several days on that food before the next hunting expedition. During the warm months, survival was assured, as the game and the weather made it easy to find food and endure the elements.

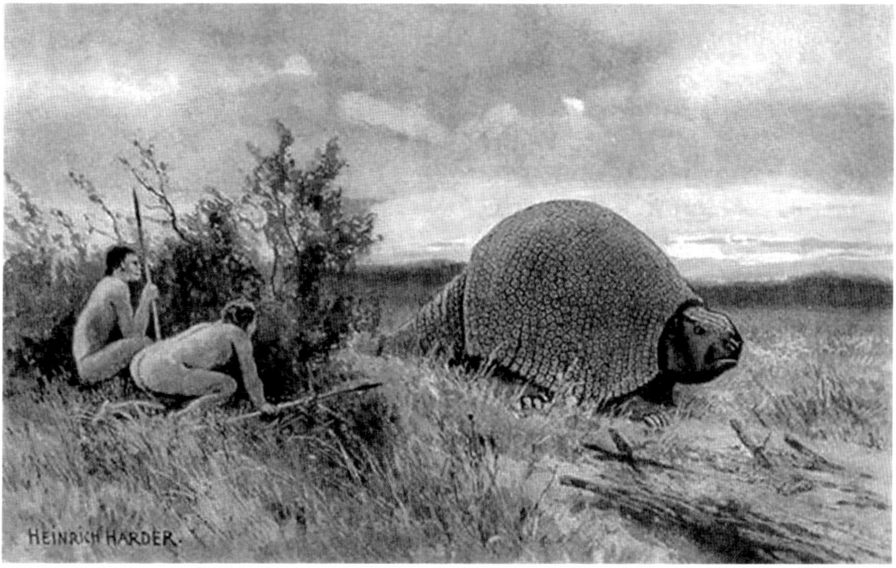

Glyptodon, one of the megafauna the early Indians would have crossed the Bering Sea to hunt. Art of Heinrich Harder (1858–1935). *Public domain.*

But the winter months were harsh, as the game hibernated or traveled long distances for warmth. The cold also brought the dangers of frostbite and freezing to death.

Around 11,500 BCE, a change in the habits of the Paleo-Indians can be identified. In what is called the Clovis period, the Indians—having been in the land for several generations—knew what foods could be foraged, harvested and stored. So they became foragers. Because of the growing extinction of the megafauna, they changed to hunting smaller animals such as rabbits, squirrels and beaver. They also hunted aquatic animals and ate the plants they found in different areas.

The Clovis Indians made tools with ivory and bone, but they are unique in that the Clovis pointed spear ends were fluted on each side. The serrated edges were deadlier because of their ability to tear into flesh more easily. The increased hunting success of the Paleo-Indians made their treks for food shorter. As they no longer followed the megafauna herds around, their range of travel began to narrow down to areas much like preserves for most of the year. Although they did still engage in month-long hunting expeditions, they became more seasonal nomads.

The Clovis people and others like them were a bridge into the Archaic period, from 8,000 to 2,000 BCE. The climate was warming. Due to

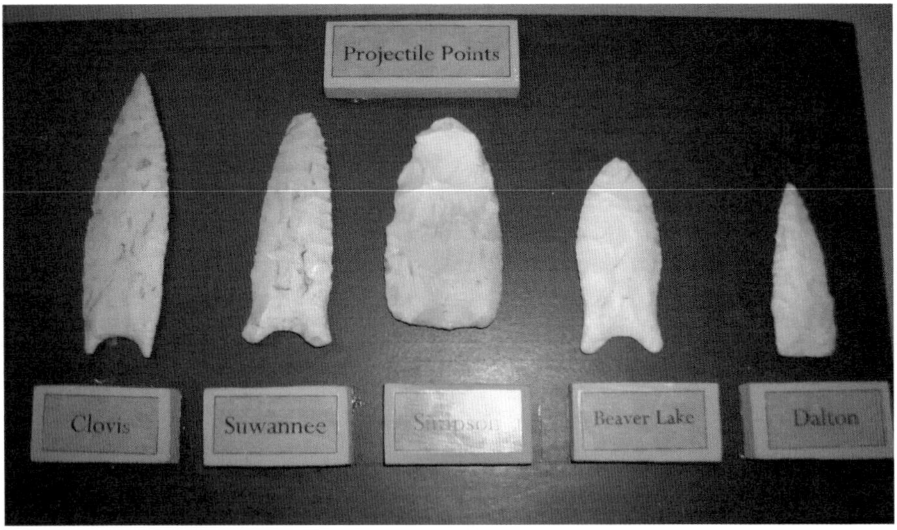

Clovis projectile point with other discovered projectile points. *Author's collection.*

successful hunting, the last of the megafauna disappeared. Mammoths and giant sloths no longer roamed the land. Because they were now localized and not constantly nomadic people, regional cultures and traditions began to develop. The environment of a Southwest Indian was different from that of an Arctic Indian. The flora and fauna were different. The seasons varied in length and severity. Available types of materials for tools and housing were different.

Now that they traded a nomadic life for a more settled existence, their economy became mixed and not centered on hunting alone. They knew the seasonally wild vegetables and fruits in their areas. They discovered the different local small game and fish; therefore, distinctive diets of different regions were established. They were now hunters *and* gatherers. Because they were able to study over time the animals in their regions, they became more sophisticated hunters and fishers. Fish weirs, or traps, were developed, structures built of stone, reeds or wooden posts placed within a stream to direct or herd fish into basketry netting or wattle fences. This greatly increased their fish harvest.

The Archaic Indians also began the process of the domestication of New World plants such as gourds, maize and cassava (beans). These three groups of plants later became the cherished Three Sisters of corn, squash and beans. The Archaic period saw the development of earthworks, the first American pottery and even wells.

This period was followed by the Woodland period, which stretched from 1000 BCE to 1000 CE. Pottery and its technological advancement and distinctiveness from one group to another was a marker of the period. Pottery forms, decorations and manufacturing practices help identify where a piece was made and who produced it.

The advancement of agriculture caused more and more people to permanently live in villages and cities. Nuts such as hickory and acorns were now processed, harvested and preserved in large amounts for immediate use and during the winters. They built storehouses, which were not useful for nomadic people who might or might not return to a given place. Wild blueberries, raspberries and strawberries were included in their diets.

Because of the need for more permanent housing, abodes such as longhouses were built. The longhouses could be over two hundred feet long, twenty-five feet wide and twenty-five feet high. They had fireplaces and fire pits that ran down the middle. Many families shared these structures. Each family was given a campfire or fire pit for warmth and cooking.

As agricultural knowledge increased crop variations, the Woodland Indians no longer needed corn from neighboring towns. The need to trade for a variety of foods decreased. The people became isolated and stayed closer to home; thus, distinctive towns and villages were started. Small-scale cultures emerged in the various communities. Most of these communities were developed near rivers and creeks for easy access to water and fish. The water made traveling easier and faster as they developed their canoes and other aquatic vessels.

By the end of the Woodland period, a great agricultural society had developed. This period is known as the Mississippian period and developed around 1000–1400 CE. This society may have been the Indians with whom the Europeans first came into contact five hundred years later.

When the Indians left the decimated Mississippian culture villages (a topic to be discussed later), they entered the Southeast and, specifically, the Georgia area; they would have encountered the remains of the Spanish mission Indians and the Guales. To make room for themselves, they had to carve out—through battles with the Indians who currently lived there—land for themselves. These new Native Americans came from the more advanced Mississippian cultures. They were more organized and appeared to easily displace the Indians already there. They became known as the Creeks. One of the reasons the Creeks were successful in conquering most of Georgia and Alabama was that they incorporated the Indians they conquered in their loose confederation of towns. But first, let us pause a moment and look

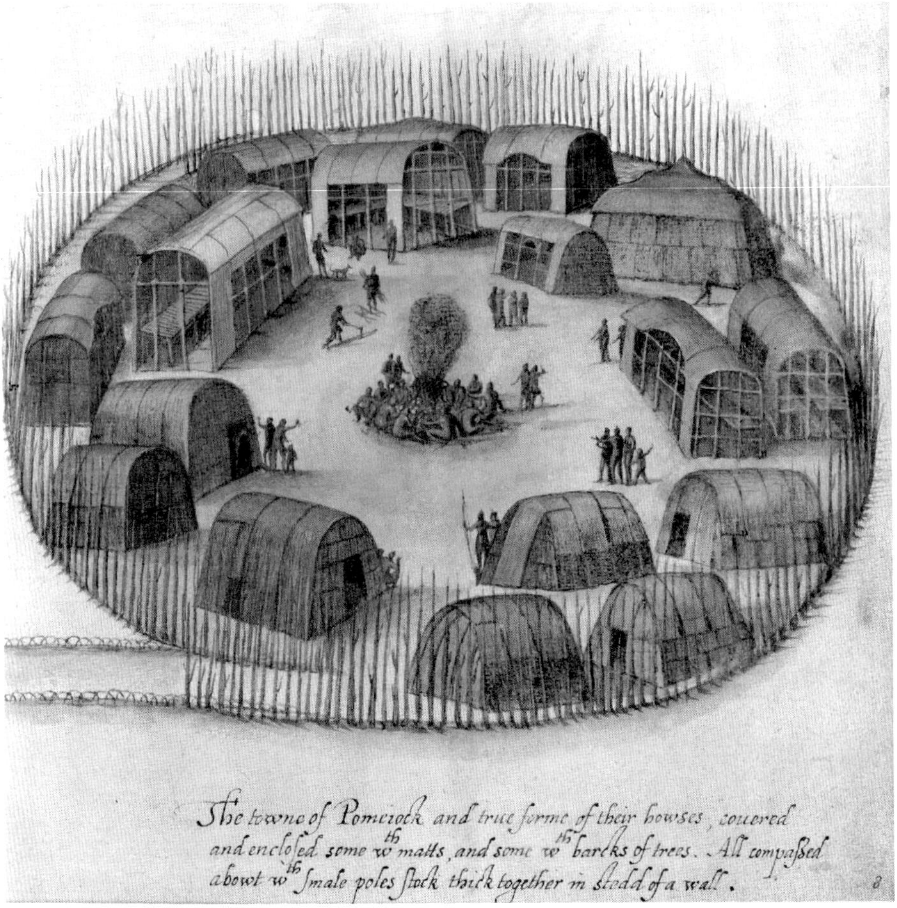

A Woodland Indian village. Illustration by John White (1540–1593). *Public domain.*

at the Woodland Indian cultures and Spanish mission Indians who were in the area when these new people came to Georgia.

Let us for a moment examine the two different groups of Indians that met in Georgia. They came to the southeastern United States from two separate places. The first came from a group that, after crossing the Bering Sea, did not stop for any significant time in the Southwest but continued eastward. They were nomadic and chose not to stay. Some of these Indians would create one of America's great civilizations: the Mississippian culture (which we will talk about later in greater detail). The Mississippian culture clustered in cities and made extensive use of agriculture. The second group included those who traveled from Europe to the Northeast United States.

They did not stop along the way either but continued to wander until they came to the Southeast. As they were nomadic, they did not have cultural traditions as refined as those of people who settled and lived in cities, daily sharing ideas and creating different customs.

The former Mississippian Indians encountered the European Indians who had already populated the land, overtook them in battle and culturally subsumed them. As they came from large cities, the Mississippians were more organized and used to working together. Any time two cultures meet, both will come away influenced by the other. In the time of the settling of South Carolina and Georgia, several different cultures developed; the most prominent in Georgia were known as the Creeks.

2

GUALES ON A MISSION

The Spanish had a firm foothold on the eastern coast of the United States by the late sixteenth century. When fifty-one Scots settled in Port Royal in 1684, by 1686, the Spanish had destroyed the settlement. Juan Ponce de León, the Spanish explorer, first came to Florida in 1513, looking for more slaves to work on Caribbean rice plantations. The Spanish moved from there to establish the oldest continuously occupied city in America, St. Augustine, as a fort and town in 1565. They used St. Augustine as their outpost for reaching into what we now know as Georgia and South Carolina and, if possible, all the way up the Atlantic Seaboard. Years later, this tactic was more successful on the West Coast.

The Spanish in Mexico, the southwestern United States and California created missions to spread their empire. This strategy proved successful, but before they set their sights on the West Coast, they employed these tactics on the East Coast. The East Coast missions are not as well known because of their comparatively short life spans. The Spanish idea was to send out missionaries to convert the Indians and establish mission/forts as they expanded their empire. This effort resulted in a chain of missions reaching all the way up to Tybee Island (known as Savannah's beach) from St. Augustine. They had missions on Cumberland, Sapelo and St. Catherine's Islands and some say even Port Royal, South Carolina.

The Guales (pronounced Wall-E) were the Native Americans the missionaries encountered off the Georgia coast. They were part of the Mississippian culture. Guale lived along the Georgia coast and sea islands

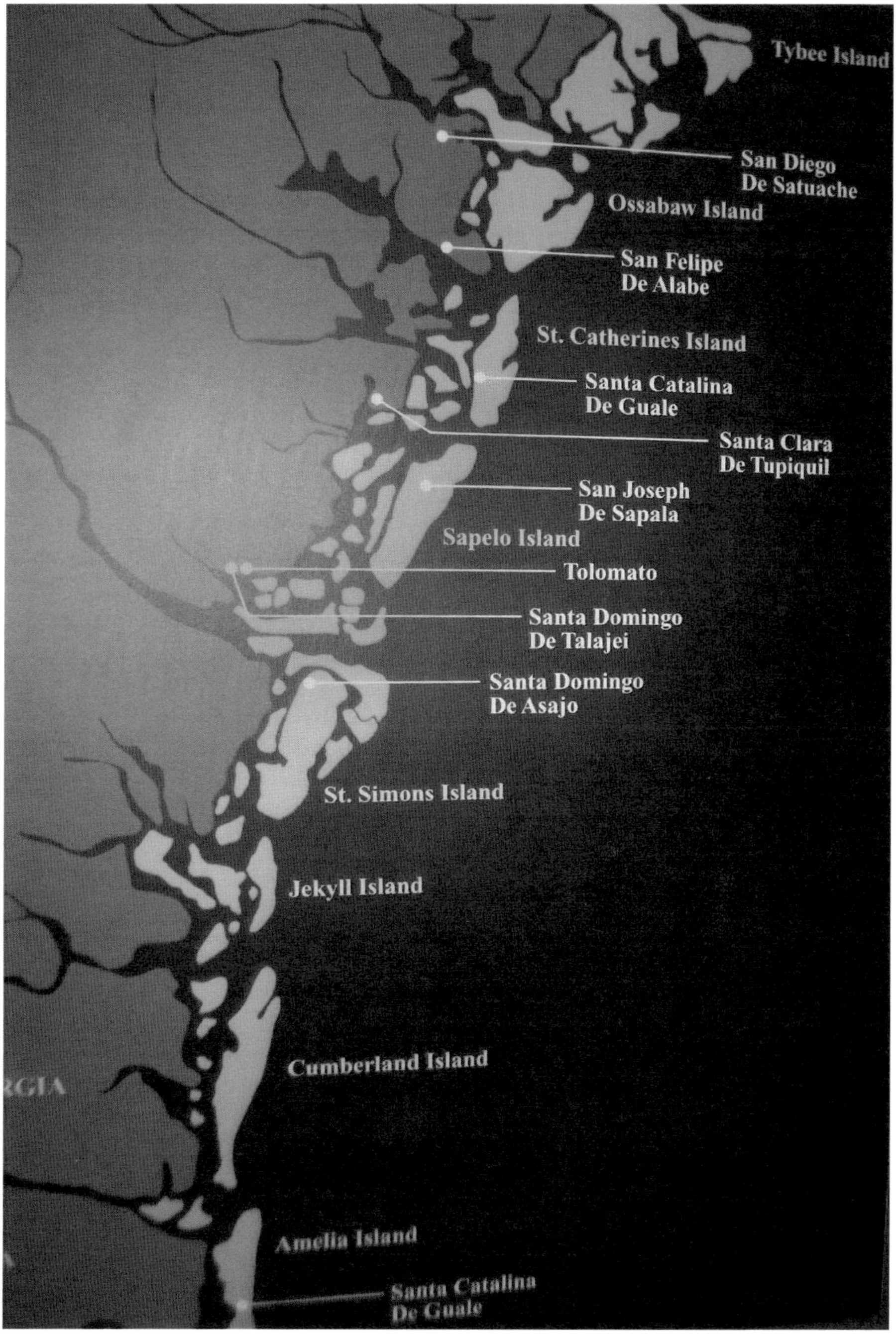

Map of Spanish missions along the coast of Florida and Georgia. *Carl Vinson Institute of Government, University of Georgia.*

from at least 1150 CE. There were two stages of Guale cultures: the first was the Savannah phase, and the second was the Irene phase, from 1300 to 1600.

In the sixteenth century, as the Spaniards were looking to spread the mission system to the north Florida and Georgia coasts, they contacted the Guale. Soon, Guale territory became one of the four primary mission provinces of Spanish Florida, each named after the tribes they encountered. The Timucua lived in northeast and north-central Florida and southeast Georgia. They were divided into thirty-five chiefdoms, some with thousands of people in them. The second group was the Mocama, part of the Ticuma Nation, who lived in the coastal areas of north Florida and south Georgia. A third group of missions was established with the Apalachee; they were primarily located on the panhandle of Florida and reached into central and southwest Georgia. They spoke a Muskogean language called Apalachee, which is now extinct. This is the area of the Creek Nation where Tomochichi lived before the Yamasee War. The fourth mission group the Spanish established was in Guale territory. They lived along the coast of present-day Georgia and the sea islands.The largest mission was on St. Catherine's Island. Although there is some evidence of Spanish mission activity on Tybee Island, nothing conclusive has been discovered. We do know that the Guales inhabited Tybee Island and all of the coastal barrier islands of Georgia.

Indians began to gather around the Guale missions in the seventeenth century. They were attracted by the Spanish and European goods. The Guales were the foothold Spain had in Georgia. But the British were advancing farther and farther south from their beginnings in Massachusetts and other northern colonies. The British in the Carolina colonies and their Westo Indian allies started pushing the Spanish out of the lower South Carolina and Georgia coastal areas. The Guale missions became the last coastal areas in Georgia not held by the British. This made the Guale missions attractive to Native Americans from north-central Georgia who traveled to Guale territory in hopes of attaining Spanish goods and escaping from the forward-pushing British. One of these groups was called *La Tama* by the Spanish. Some of the La Tama, having lost in battle with the Westo Indians, resettled near Guale missions. The Guales and these new Indians looked to the Spanish for protection. These wandering Indians became known as Yamasees.

As with any early Native American civilization, when they had close contact with the Europeans, they encountered disease. The Guale numbered about 4,000 at the height of their civilization. Aggressive attacks by the Westo and disease from their Spanish neighbors took a terrible toll on their lives. It was the Westo tribe that had caused the diaspora of the La Tama. The British colonists had decided the Spanish influence was too close for comfort, so the British colony of Carolina backed the Westo as they destroyed the Spanish mission system in Georgia. By 1684, the Guale Nation had been removed, and the Guales were pushed into Florida. The once powerful Guale population diminished to 1,215 by 1715. Some of the scattered remnants of Guale and Yamassee became known as one entity: the Yemassees. This new configuration of the Yemassees stayed in Georgia but broke ties with the Spanish, who had not provided security from the British and Westoes. They now aligned themselves with the British.

The Guales, a Mississippian tribe that once lived on the coast of Savannah and Georgia, have long since vanished. Yet when you speak the names of Tybee, Ossabaw and Sapelo Islands, you hear the faint echo of the Guales who once lived there.

3

THE MISSISSIPPIAN CULTURE WAS A BIG DEAL

The Mississippians were a part of the Mound Builders, who were inhabitants of North America for five centuries. They can be found in the Archaic period—well before Columbus arrived—in the Woodland period and the Mississippian culture period. The Mound Builders culture existed from 3500 BCE until the sixteenth century CE, when Hernando de Soto encountered them in his rampage through the Southeast. They were located near water sources such as the Great Lakes, Ohio River Valley and, of course, the Mississippi River Valley.

The Mound Builders seemed to be a conglomeration of two groups of Woodland Indians: one that had not stopped in the West after crossing the Bering Sea and another that came from Europe. The Woodland Indians met the wandering members of the Southwest and Mexican Native American cultures and became what we call the Mound Builders.

The Mound Builders had in common the construction of flat-topped pyramids (similar to ones in Mexico), or as some call them, platform mounds. These mounds took various shapes: some were rounded cones, others ridges and some even the shape of animals. They were built as part of a town complex. The earliest of these mounds can be found in Louisiana and date to 3500 BCE; the Louisiana mounds are the only ones known to be built by a hunter-gatherer culture. Towns capable of this magnitude of work come from agriculturalists as a rule.

The Mississippian culture was a much later and grander society that existed from 900 to 1450 CE. This culture spread through the eastern

United States. The capital of the Mississippians was a city that rivaled—in size—any European city of its day: Cahokia.

Cahokia was the largest town in the United States; at its height, the population was between 10,000 and 15,300. The original site contained 120 earthen mounds over an area of six square miles. A huge complex of this size would have required thousands of workers moving incomprehensible sums of dirt using woven baskets—for decades. Think of it this way: one fourteen-acre mound is one hundred feet tall. On top of that mound was a five-thousand-square-foot building yet another fifteen feet high.

At Cahokia, located in Illinois, you will find many of the characteristics found in the Mississippians, including the pyramid mounds with chiefs' homes built on top, along with other ceremonial buildings. The villagers were agriculturalists, and their primary crop was maize. Both the Southwest Indians and the Mississippians created different hybrids of corn to fit the different environments and taste, one of the many amazing aspects of their cultures. This hybridization process developed well before Gregor Mendel and his peas in the nineteenth century. The Native Americans' expertise in growing corn helped create large fields able to sustain huge populations living in cities.

The huge gardens and farmland enabled huge populations to live in proximity with each other. Each town had ceremonial buildings and mounds serving as regional centers. Eventually, they became too large and hard to support. When this happened, smaller towns were developed—much like our modern suburbs—they may have had their own communities but were tied to the larger population centers.

It was with the moving from the nomadic life to a settled city life that pottery of different types came into profuse use. Each city developed its own particular style, and because the societies were established next to waterways, they often shared styles over regions. The Mississippian Indians created social hierarchies; chiefdoms became hereditary, not positions of meritocracy. Part of this institutionalization included power in the hands of an elite class. The particular town one hailed from increased one's power and status among elite and common alike. People, as we do today, give more credence to Atlanta versus Mayberry elites. The chiefs, by placing their homes on top of the mounds and in the more important cities, were literally put in a higher plane than others. All of this would have been enhanced by an adoption of ceremonial space and practice. The Ocmulgee Village in Macon, Georgia's Earth Lodge, personified the class nature of the Mississippians. The conical lodge has a dark, narrow entrance that one must duck to enter. Inside the

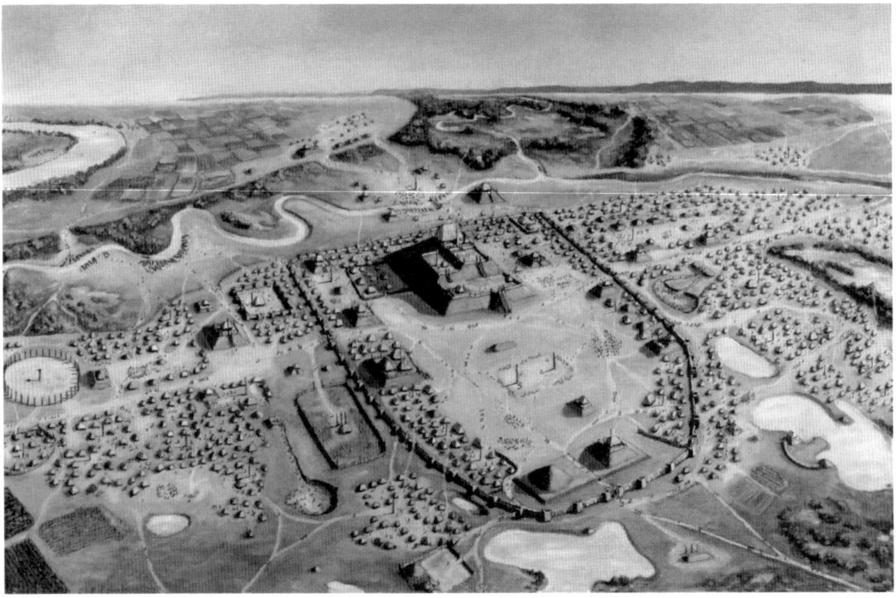

Cahokia, the largest Mississippian Indian village. *William R. Iseminger.*

lodge is a petroglyph of an eagle molded out of clay on the floor. Around the eagle was a semicircle with carved seats in the clay floor. The seats on the end were smaller and lower and steadily grew and rose as they came to the center. In the center was the largest and highest seat in the lodge. It was, of course, the chief's.

The ritual game of chunkey came into existence around 600 CE in the Cahokia region. Chunkey was played in huge arenas, some over forty acres with space for audiences to come and watch together. This was, in many ways, like the Roman gladiators of the past entertaining the masses in huge arenas. The game was played by rolling a large stone disc across the field and seeing who could throw a spear closest to the disc. People gambled on their favorite players, and chunkey was taken very seriously. Another source of reinforcement of the culture was the creation of myths, expressed in art and religious articles.

Because the Mississippian culture and influence spread up to Wisconsin and from Louisiana through Georgia and Alabama, there were several distinctive groups. One of these was the South Appalachian Mississippian variant. This group included many sites in Georgia, including Moundville, Etowah, Ocmulgee and, five miles outside of Savannah, the Irene Complex. It is believed Irene was the only site close to the coast.

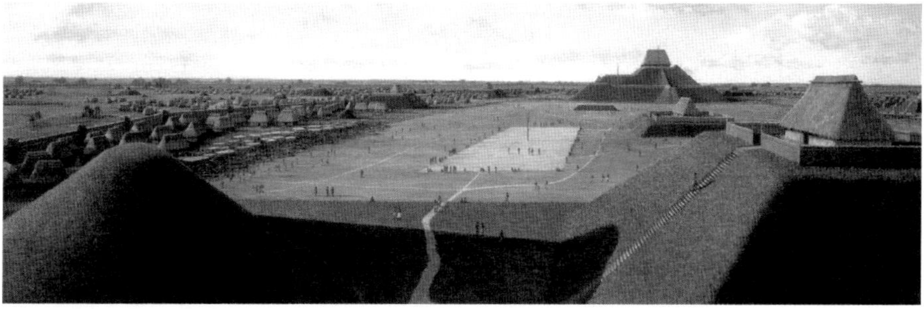

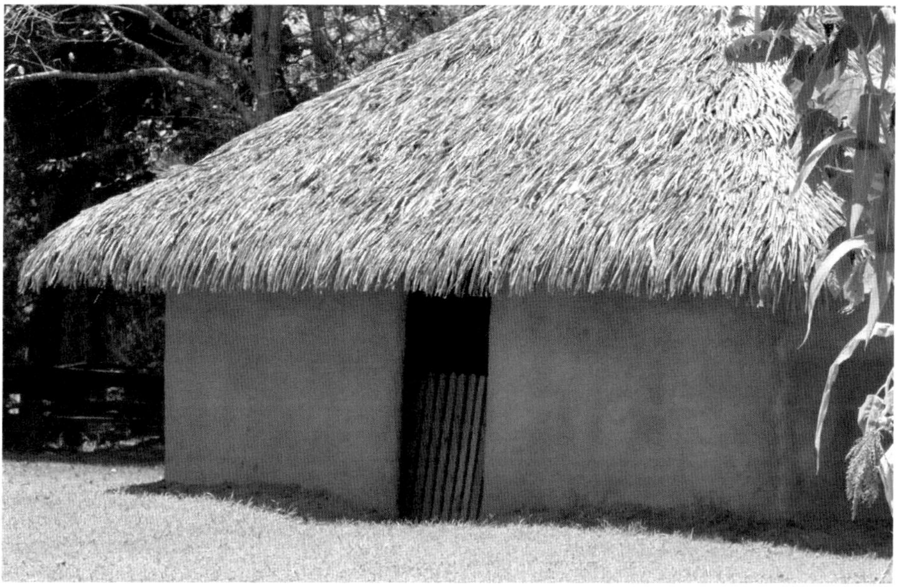

Top: The Grand Square, where stickball and other community events would have occurred. *Lloyd K. Townsend.*

Bottom: A recreation of the homes of Mississippian Indians. *Author's collection.*

Now that the people had become more sedentary, there was more time for crafts and artistic expression, especially, as discussed earlier, in their pottery. The Mississippian towns had contact and creative interactions with many other Indians, as their trade routes were expansive. They traded as far west as the Rockies, north to the Great Lakes, south to the Gulf of Mexico and east to the Atlantic Ocean.

The cities with mounds and more development dominated smaller and less developed cities. The cities developed a stratified culture with chiefs and other elites, who often lived on top of mounds. To unify people spread across

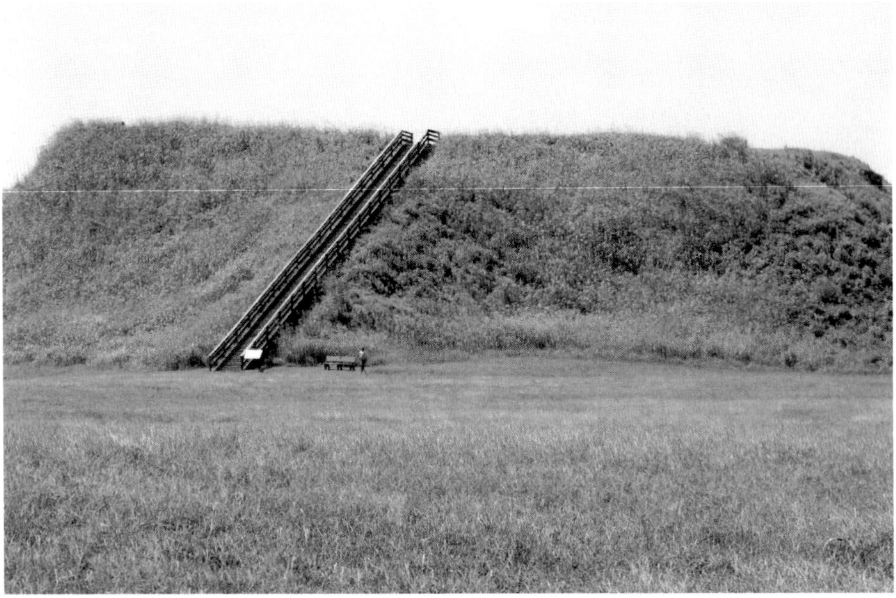

The main Etowah Village mound. *Author's collection.*

such vast geography, a central religious and civil authority developed. To hold all the cities and peoples together, ceremonies and rituals were created to galvanize and indoctrinate the peoples. De Soto arrived at the end of the Mississippian culture, when the great society was in decay and a new way of life was emerging. Yet even he noticed the Native Americans were not an uncivilized people.

The people of the Irene Mounds outside of Savannah were the easternmost town of the Mississippian culture. They lived between 1100 and 1600 CE. They had a complex of several mounds, made pottery and traded with towns from a great distance. They had their own hierarchical culture. They had ceremonies that, for the most part, were practiced throughout the Mississippian reign. They would have, of course, grown what is called the Three Sisters—corn, beans and squash—but because of their proximity to the ocean, they also ate fish and shellfish.

The Irene Mounds were located five miles northwest of Savannah. They were built on the Savannah River and surrounded on two sides by small creeks. On the third side, they constructed a small ditch. As was customary of the Mississippians, the village included several mounds. The largest, which would have been the temple mound, was rectangular and

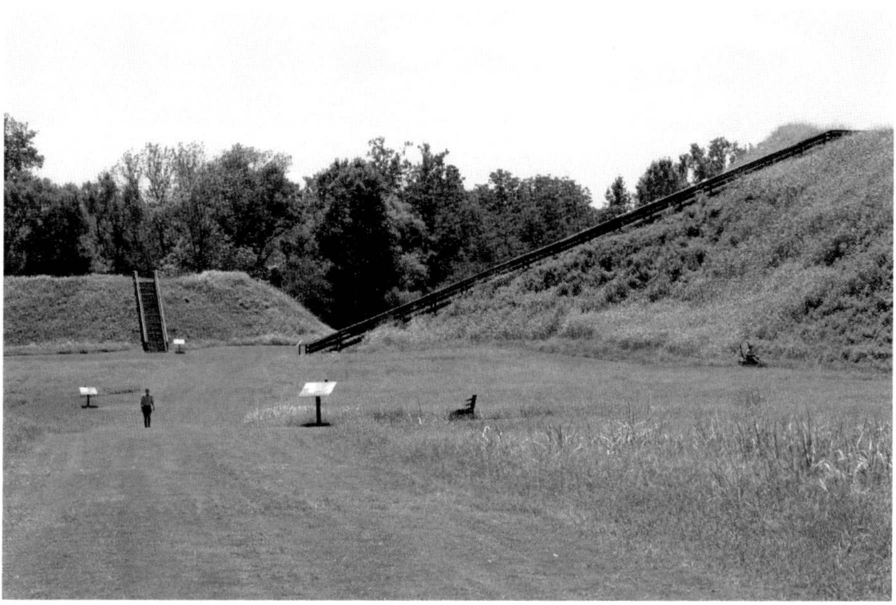

The main Etowah Village mound and a lesser mound. *Author's collection.*

flat-topped. This structure was accompanied by a small conical mound and a burial mound.

On the ground surrounding these mounds would have been a square building used for the chief's communal and business meetings. In the middle of all the homes and communal buildings would have stood a rotunda for gatherings and the playing of games. The Irene Mounds were thought to be for the chief and religious purposes. So the village probably only had as residents the chief and members of his family, estimated anywhere between thirty and forty people. The settlement was a touchstone for all of the neighboring Indians, as well as those who were traveling hunters from deeper south or west Georgia. This place was one Tomochichi would have thought of when he talked about wanting to return to the sacred ground of his ancestors. The religious ceremonies once held there and the burial grounds still there made it a sacred place for the Indians of Tomochichi's time.

The site has a unique history in more ways than one. In September 1937, the Irene Mounds were excavated by archaeologists and forty-seven African American women. The project was part of President Franklin D. Roosevelt's New Deal Program, the Works Progress Administration (WPA). The fact that

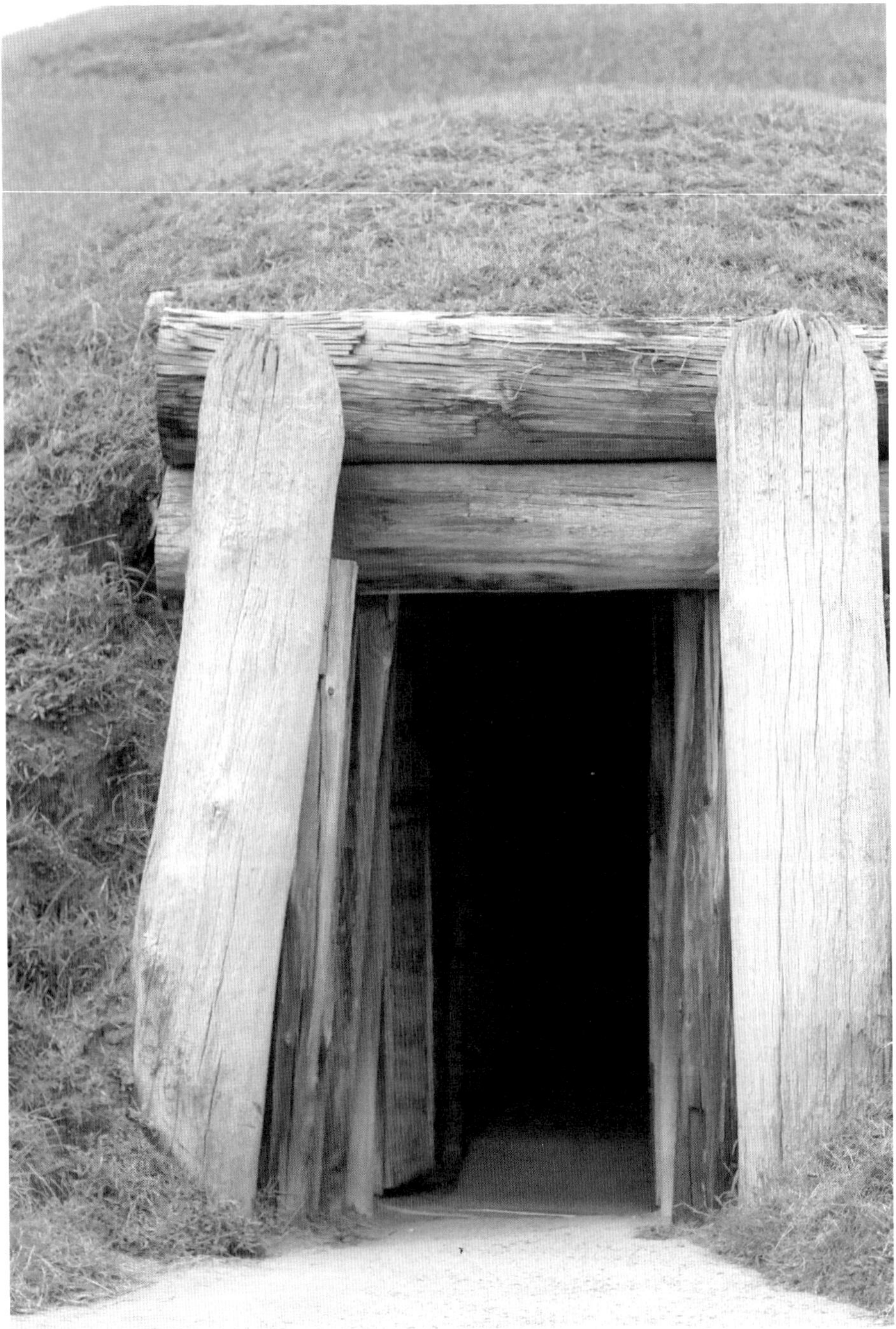

Entrance to Ocmulgee Village's one-thousand-year-old earth lodge. *Author's collection.*

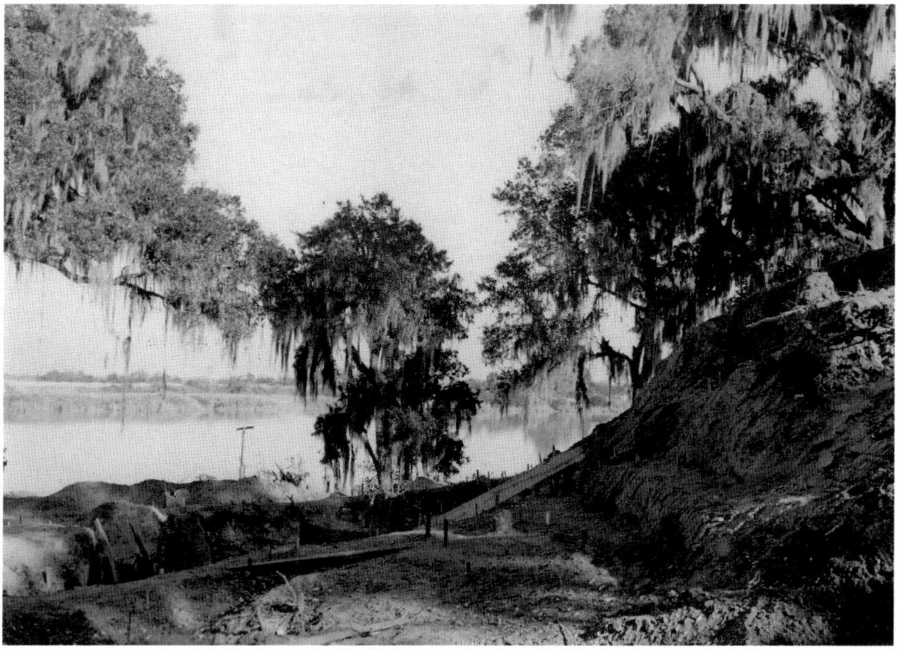

Part of an excavated Irene Village mound. *Courtesy of Georgia Historical Society.*

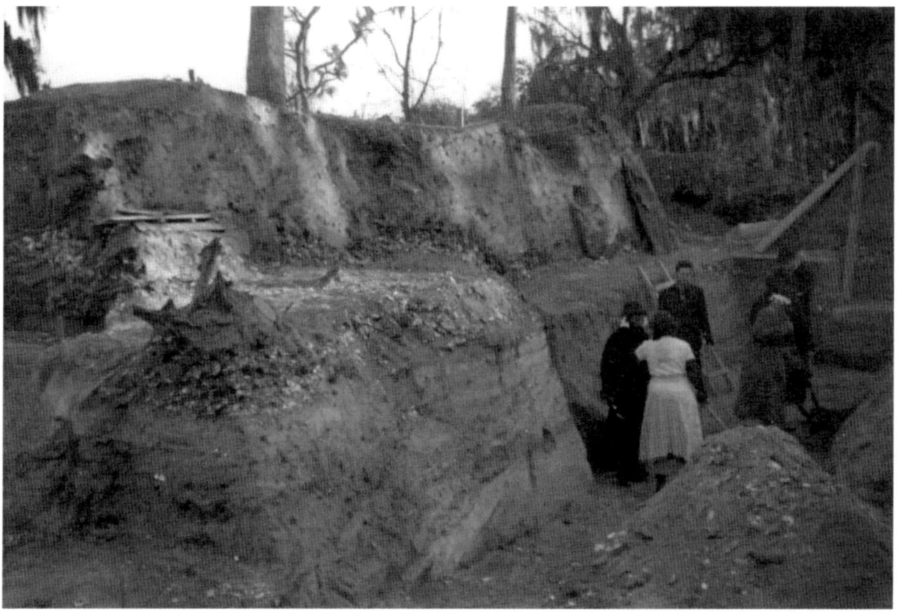

Picture of WPA African American women working on Irene Village mounds. *Courtesy of Georgia Historical Society.*

educated black women were hired for the job broke several taboos. First, the hard, physical work of excavation was thought not to be the sphere of women. Second, black women were excluded from many of the New Deal's work programs, especially in the South. The site excavation became quite the story, with regular updates on the work by the *Savannah Morning News* in 1937 and 1938. Schoolchildren were taken to the site as an educational outing. The fact that these black women were educated helped with the site excavation, according to several of the archaeologists.

One of the biggest discoveries was that the Irene inhabitants appeared to have and perhaps even created a form of pottery in the Swift Creek tradition. This style of pottery is made with paddles with engraved designs that were then pressed into a clay pot before firing. The designs were often complex curvilinear patterns. This unique style is found at both the Ocmulgee and Etowah Mounds in Georgia and even in a few places in neighboring states.

Irene Mounds were named after a small mission and school for the Indians established by the Moravians at the request of Tomochichi in 1736. The remnants of the school were located on the summit of the temple mound during the 1930s excavations, thus the name. Today, the site is completely destroyed and lies under the ship docks of the Georgia Ports Authority.

The Irene Mounds' population was what James B. Griffin termed "South Appalachian Mississippian culture, a subculture of the vast Mississippian culture." This included villages in Alabama, Georgia, northern Florida, South Carolina, central and western North Carolina and Tennessee. Etowah and Ocmulgee are two such towns in Georgia. The images provided here of mounds in Etowah and Ocmulgee are indicative of the mounds at the Irene Mounds.

Unlike Irene, one of the major problems that large centers like Cahokia faced was keeping a steady supply of food. A related problem was waste disposal for the dense population. Cahokia became unhealthy from polluted waterways. Because it was such an unhealthy place to live, some believe that the town had to rely on social and political attractions to bring in a steady supply of new immigrants; otherwise, the town's death rate would have caused it to be abandoned even earlier.

We can see some of the reasons of the demise of the Mississippian culture by looking at the waning of Cahokia. The site began to decline during the thirteenth century, and the site was eventually abandoned around 1300. Many scholars have proposed environmental factors, such as over-hunting, deforestation and flooding, as explanations. As the cities used up the

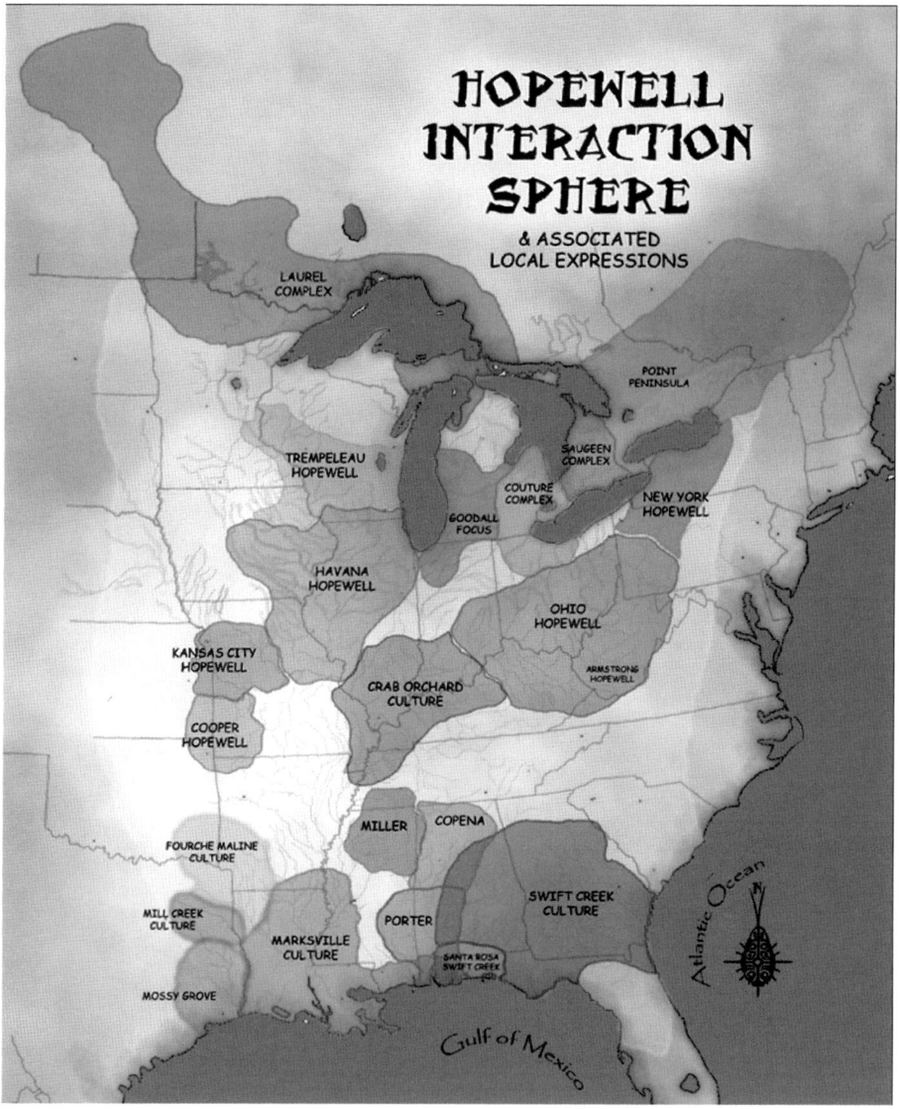

Map showing the Hopewell culture influence. *Herb Roe, Creative Commons.*

surrounding trees and game, residents had to travel farther and farther from their hometowns for resources. This eventually created a lack of allegiance to the large cities and a joining of smaller, more manageable villages.

It is likely that diseases were transmitted in the large, dense cities, prompting people to flee from them. It also appears that severe floods

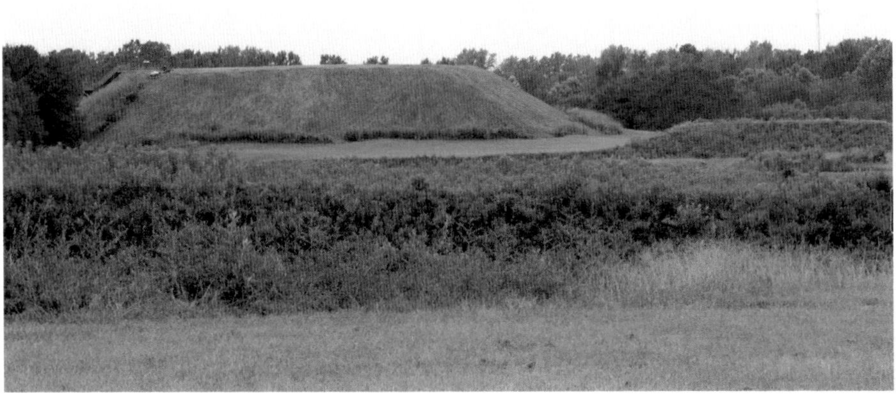

The main Ocmulgee Village mound. *Author's collection.*

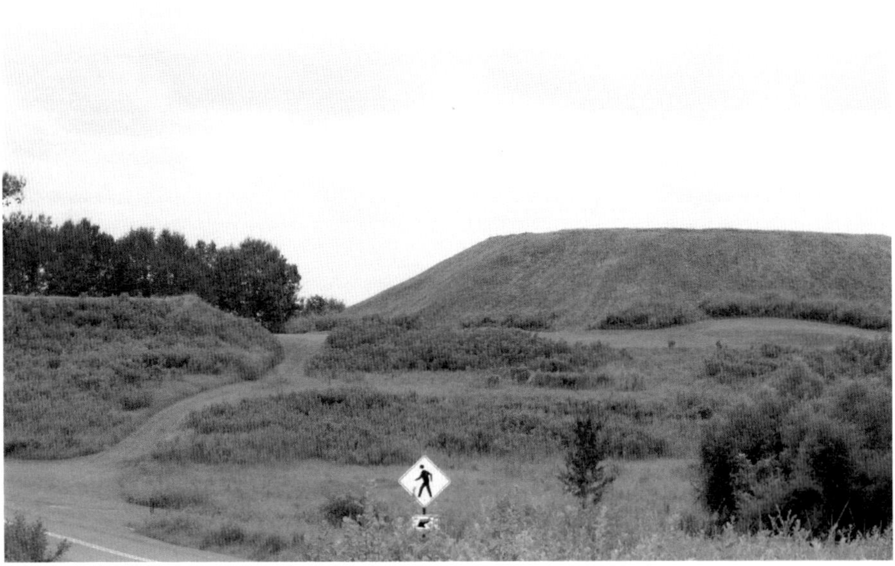

Another mound at Ocmulgee Village. *Author's collection.*

inundated the cities, leading to Cahokia's decline. All of these factors may have played an important part in the ending of the Mississippian civilizations. The Mississippian era ended around 1600 CE.

Whatever the cause of the demise of the Mississippian culture, by the time Tomochichi and other Native Americans came to the Savannah area, they were gone. The only traces left were the mounds and some of their cultural influences on the Creeks and other Indians. But the Irene Mounds are what Tomochichi would have referred to when he spoke of his ancestors inhabiting the Savannah area.

4

THE YAMASEE WAR WAS THE CREEK VIETNAM WAR

The Yamasee War was a long time coming and the eventual turning point for the Creek Nation. It had an impact similar to the Vietnam War's in the United States. Just as the Vietnam War did, the Yamasee War left the Creeks with questions about the efficacy of war, how they were to be in the world at large with the colonists with whom they now lived and what their place in this new world would be.

When Barbados plantation owners first came to settle in the new Carolina colony and created the city of Charleston, they brought with them slaves and an attitude of English superiority. The English determined that the clearing of Native Americans from the land by disease was God's way of preparing the way for them—a not quite fully developed concept of Manifest Destiny, which was promoted in the 1900s. The colonists primarily viewed the Native Americans as tools to build their trade and fortune. As long as the Indians met their needs, they maintained a certain amount of consideration. These needs diminished as the settlers became more ensconced in the New World. At first, the Indians were useful as trade partners for food, a source of forced labor and deerskins. The food trade dwindled as the settlers developed farmland of their own. As the colonists desired more land for an agricultural economy, the natives became a nuisance or, even worse, a threat. The African slave trade devalued the usefulness of Indian labor and also enabled the settlers to work even more land. Colonists' attitudes toward the Indians changed. Meanwhile, the Native Americans became angry with the slow but steady encroachment on their land. Unlike the Native Americans, whose oversight of the land was communal, the settlers' use of the land was for personal gain. The Indians used the land as a great game preserve, and the colonists used the land to grow crops for their livelihood. This meant when a settler homesteaded, the property could no longer be used by the Indians. Yet when Indians controlled land, it remained in the hands of a tribe and their allies to use. But because the land was not tended and used seasonally, it was open to encroachment by the settlers.

Deerskins were all the fashion in Europe. Cotton was steadily taking hold in Europe and eventually became the primary crop of the colonists in the Deep South. But deerskins remained valuable trade items until the advent of the cotton gin on the Mulberry Grove Plantation outside of Savannah on March 14, 1794. Mulberry Grove Plantation was granted to General Nathanael Greene, the Revolutionary War hero of the southern front of that war. Greene died soon after, but his wife, known as Caty, maintained the farm. It would be Caty who extended the fateful invitation to Eli Whitney to visit Mulberry Grove. There, Whitney worked on and eventually improved and enhanced the cotton gin and the cotton industry as a whole. This technological advance and changing fashions in Europe decreased the need for trade with the Indians for deerskins and increased the settlers' need for land to grow cotton. The Native Americans traded more and more for guns, and the deer population in the area began to dwindle. This caused Native Americans, who were accustomed to the British goods, to go into unpayable amounts of debt to unscrupulous traders, who often took payment forcibly—in the form of enslavement of the Indians.

The other need, as far as the Carolinians were concerned, besides slaves for work, was soldiers to protect the borders. The British could cut the cost of their security needs significantly if they kept the Indians as allies. The Native Americans served as buffers between the French in the west and the Spanish in the south as long as they were allies with the British.

The Indians' claim to the land was a great hindrance to the continual western push of the colonies. At the same time, Native Americans were no longer needed for slaves. One of the reasons the Africans made better slaves was they did not know the land. This made them unlikely to run away. In contrast, it was easy for Native Americans to disappear, because family and familiar territory were near. A further consternation for the colonists was some tribes took in runaway slaves, and this became a thorn in the side of the slave owners. As long as the Native Americans were a nation inside of a nation or a wall preventing westward expansion, they were perceived as a threat to the colonists.

The Yamasees, as noted earlier, were originally refugees fleeing the British and Westo into Guale land. Where they had once been loyal to the Spanish, they turned their loyalty to the British. Some of the Guale from Florida left to get out from under the Spanish control in several migrations. In 1687, Spaniards attempted to send Yamasees to the West Indies as slaves, and the tribe moved into South Carolina. The Spanish used the Yamasees as slaves to help build their fort at St. Augustine. Meanwhile, the British made raids of Yamasee lands for supplies and slaves while the Spanish stood impotently by, unable to stop them. In 1708 alone, the Carolinians captured from ten to twelve thousand Native Americans. These events caused the Yamasees, even those in Florida, to decide the settlers of Carolina were a better bet for survival—so they switched sides. The Yamasees quickly developed ties with the British colony and would be influential in the Tuscarora War of 1711. The Tuscarora tribes from the northern Iroquois Nation were fighting with a coalition to oust the colonists. The Yamasees and Cherokees, whose land was also being encroached on by the northern tribes, fought on the side of the British to expel the Tuscarora from the land. The Tuscarora had gone to war over the colonists' pushing them farther south and capturing hundreds of them for slavery. The Tuscarora lost, and most rejoined their Iroquois brothers and sisters in the north. This should have been a foreshadowing for the Yamasees of what would happen to them. But for the time being, they found they liked the British trade goods, which were more abundant and of better quality than the Spanish or French. This new relationship seemed to work for nearly fifteen years.

The British enjoyed the relationship because of the previously mentioned trade benefits, but they also saved money by not building forts in the western interior of South Carolina and the southern interior of Georgia. Because of the friendly relations with the Yamasees, Cherokees and Creeks, they concentrated on building forts on the coastal areas and left their southern and western flanks protected by the Native Americans. In 1702, Queen Anne's War broke out between the British and Spanish in Europe. In America, the Spanish in Florida decided that the war was a good time to advance on the British in Carolina. The Creeks turned back the Spanish at the Flint River. Furthermore, the Creeks, in 1704, cleared out the Apalachee, a troublesome foe of the colonists, from the Florida Panhandle. This act created a larger border between the Spanish and French, who had settled in Mobile, Alabama, in 1699. This action helped the British see the Creeks as valuable partners against the Spanish and French, so they joined in a pact with them in 1705.

However, after a time, the British became firmly established and no longer were as dependent on the Indians. In 1707, the British licensed Creek slave traders. This would begin a period of growing animosity between the Native Americans and the British. The Carolina government not only began to promote and license the Creek slave trade, but it also continually refused to address licensed colonist traders in general, who were abusing Native Americans more and more. Finally, when the colonists began to move into the interior of the Carolinas and settle on Creek land—despite treaties prohibiting this activity—the Upper Creeks had enough and joined forces with the Yamasees, who had experienced similar grievances. In 1715, the Yamasee War began.

At the onset of war, the colonists found themselves in a difficult situation. Because they had treaties with the Creeks and other Native Americans, they had not built forts in the west to protect their land and the city of Charleston. All of their military might had been concentrated on the coast to keep the Spanish from marauding and invading. This threat was real; on several occasions, the Spanish had made such expeditions. The other difficulty was that the Carolinas had created a rivalry with their close British neighbors to the north, Virginia. The colonies were at odds because the Carolina colonies had taken the southern Indians' trade from Virginia. So when the Carolinas made pleas for help, Virginia—which could not outright refuse assistance to another colony—instead chose to delay assistance for over a year. Officials claimed procedural matters took them time to take the formal vote before assistance could be provided. They were not refusing to aid their neighbors, they just did not have time to vote on how many troops to send and who would lead them. Even worse, Virginia offered the Carolinas' potential Native American allies, the Cherokees, incentives such as blankets, guns and other supplies to stay out of the war. The Carolinas also underestimated their opponents. The Westos, a former Native American foe, had previously held the land the Yamasees now possessed. When they became a nuisance, they were readily dispatched from the land. Of course, this was accomplished with the help of other Indian tribes. But now, no Indian tribe stood with the colonists. They probably assumed if they ever had any trouble with the replacement tribe, they could once again easily rid themselves of any new Native American threat.

All of these factors led to disaster for the colonists. When the hostilities started, the Yamasees declared war, and all of the tribes in the Southeast joined forces (including the Upper Creeks) to eradicate the British from the land. The Carolina colonists were so outnumbered they did the unthinkable and armed slaves to help in their defense. One can assume that the slaves were less than vigorous soldiers in this fight.

The settlers in the frontiers of the Carolinas evacuated to Charleston, the only city with a reliable military force. But because of the numbers of people who fled to Charleston, starvation set in as supplies ran low. The survival of the South Carolina colony was in question during 1715. The war became bloodier than the horrible northeastern conflict with Native Americans known as King Philip's War, which is often cited among North America's bloodiest wars. The war was fast becoming out of hand; in the end, 7 percent of the white citizenry were killed. The Yamasees and their partners even came perilously close to Charleston. The native combatants were twelve miles from the city before they were halted. They were stopped for two reasons: supplies and weapons came from Virginia and England and, more significantly, the Cherokees decided to side with the colonists after sitting on the sidelines at first.

The war proved the inevitability of the British colonies' power over the Creeks, and even though they had used the Cherokees to assist in their victory, it was evident that they were here to stay. A question remained: if they were here to stay, would the Creeks choose to continue in ultimately futile wars with the British, or would they find another way? One of the ways the Creeks responded was to strengthen the Creek Confederation so that they would have greater power to war if necessary or greater diplomatic power by speaking in a unified voice. They had found, just as the thirteen colonies would later, a loose confederation was not good for security. They developed a stronger confederation, and while it enhanced their position with the British, would it be strong enough? The ground had shifted beneath them, and new ideas needed to be implemented.

5

THE CREEKS KEEP THEIR HOME FIRES BURNING

The Mississippian chiefdoms collapsed around 1400 CE. The reasons were many. Smallpox killed over 89 percent of the population. The towns died because their large size had depleted the trees and animals surrounding them, dispersing people farther and farther from the mound cities. The land's soil was exhausted from over-farming. By the end of the 1600s, the southeastern Indians began to recover and the Creeks began to rise.

The English name *Creek* was given to a people that Europeans found living alongside the rivers and creeks of Georgia and Alabama. They were the descendants of the Mississippian Indians. Another name for these Native Americans was Muskogee, which came from the language that most of the Georgia Indians used. They, too, gathered around rivers and even occupied some of the same mounds and places as the Mississippian Indians. They inhabited most of Georgia and a third of Alabama. At their peak, there were sixty towns in the confederation. But they had learned a new way of being, incorporating some of the old and creating some new in their way of life. They, unlike the Mississippians, decentralized authority. They certainly had more prominent towns but not a single town from which decrees were made. In their towns, no mounds were made; instead, communal spaces were created. They had a home fire that represented their loyalty to a particular town. Each town had one. When decisions were made that affected the confederation as a whole, the towns met and decided together. They had public squares (shaped in rectangles) where the leaders made decisions. The *mico* (chief) was elected by the leaders, not necessarily by heredity. Their elite were chosen by merit. The warriors had a voice in council meetings and were divided in to two groups: warriors who had distinguished themselves and usually younger warriors who were untested. Also in the inner circle were the beloved men, men whose wise and cogent advice had been recognized by all. Beyond this was the beloved women. Women who had distinguished themselves usually did not speak during tribal meetings but did on some occasions. Beyond them were the people who watched and saw what their tribal leaders were doing. While the mico might call a smaller meeting in his lodge to discuss delicate matters, he openly announced what he thought was best, and the council voted. Decisions were not made in secret but for all to see and judge. The day-to-day decisions not of general importance were made by the mico in the open square, where all could see. They were practicing an early form of representative democracy.

The Creeks were genius at assimilating tribes and individuals, such as traders, into their confederation. When they conquered a tribe or a tribe wished to align themselves with the Creeks, they formed towns (*talwas* is the Creek word), and these towns became part of the confederation. Individuals who came to them had to align themselves with a town. Strangers who came to them were to be housed, fed and generally taken care of. They allowed intermarriage with the Europeans. They treated these marriages as equal to their own, believing they made the tribes or Europeans allies. The Creeks was a multicultural society. Sometimes, they needed interpreters to communicate within their own confederation. The Creek Confederation became one of the most powerful forces in America.

The Creeks realized they needed, as did the Mississippians, ceremonies, symbols and rituals to hold the people together. This was realized in the home fires; a flame could be taken to a meeting by a representative to a neighboring town to add to their fire to show their unity and to remind the representative he spoke not for himself but for the town from which the home fire came. The Creeks had communal practices, such as planting and harvesting common grounds full of corn, beans and squash. The men and women worked in the fields together, and the crops were dispensed appropriately. They also were known for their festivals. Europeans commented how many festivals the Creeks had and wondered how they ever got anything done. The most important was the Green Corn Festival, a ceremony still practiced today.

The Green Corn Ceremony typically occurred in late July to early August, and the celebration lasted around a week. No one was to partake

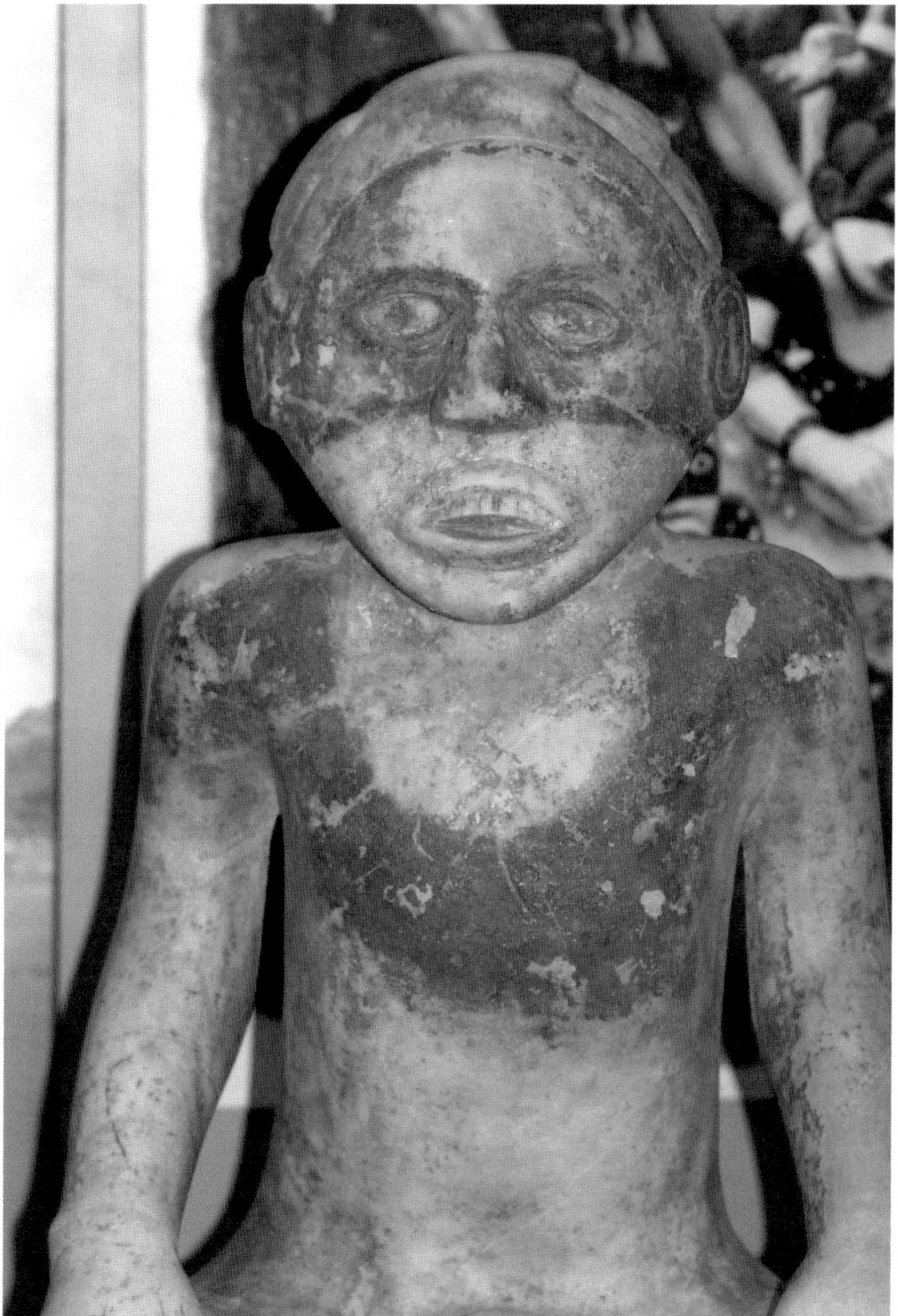

A funerary effigy found at the Etowah Mounds. *Author's collection*.

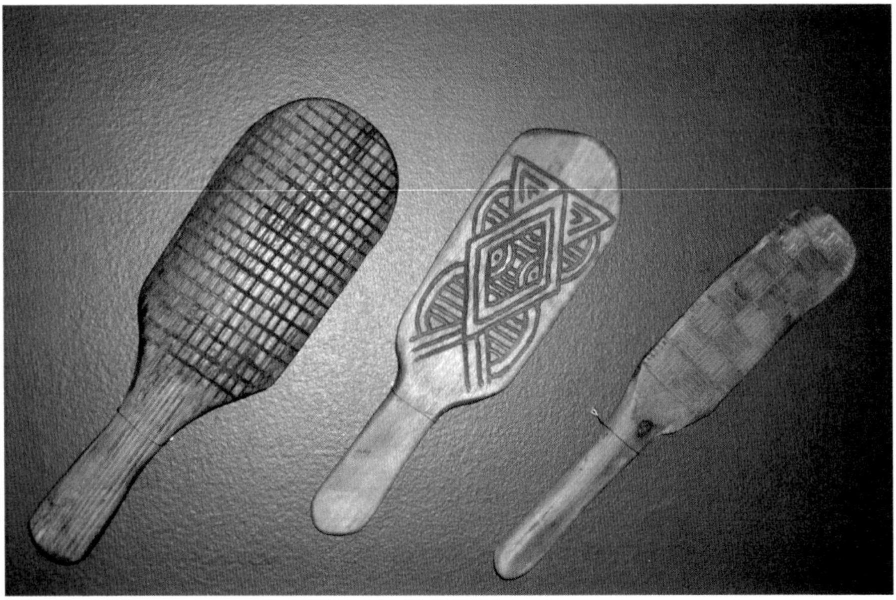

Paddles used to make imprints on pottery. *Author's collection.*

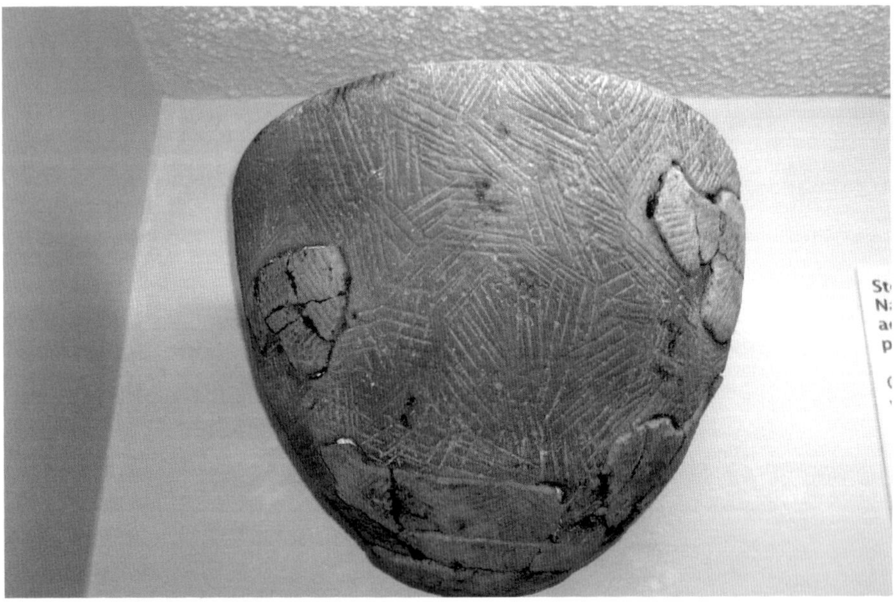

Pottery found in the Savannah area. *Author's collection.*

of harvested corn until after the festival. The town communal grounds and surrounding homes were spruced up, and the women made new clothes for the family. The men fasted and drank a mixture of yaupon holly that caused vomiting to purify themselves for the occasion. Dances in the squares, primarily by the men, were performed throughout the ceremony. Logs were placed in the middle square and lit, and everyone was to take a piece of the fire back to their abodes to light their fires. The elders gave speeches on morality. Past improprieties were forgiven. and those who had committed crimes (except murder) were welcomed back into the fold. It was a time to give young men their warrior names. Marriages were either cemented or ended. Widows could shake off their mourning period. It was part revival, part New Year celebration and part Yom Kippur. It was a time of bringing the community together, reminding all of how the Master of Breath had been kind to them and how they each belonged to their town.

The political alliance of the Creeks extended from the Ocmulgee River west to the Coosa and Tallapoosa Rivers in Alabama. They spoke a variety of languages, including Muskogee, Alabama and Hitchiti, which sometimes required interpreters to do business. But the Indian tribes and towns pledged to maintain peace with one another. They numbered about ten thousand at the time of Oglethorpe's arrival. In fact, the Creeks would not be in the minority in Georgia until the mid-1760s. When matters became tense, they would, on occasion, play a game much like modern-day lacrosse to settle issues. They used a netted racquet to pick the ball off the ground, throw, catch and convey it into or past a goal to score a point. The cardinal rule in all varieties of lacrosse was that the ball, with few exceptions, must not be touched with the hands. The towns all had fields to play the game. Because the games were often not only for pride of winning but occasionally for land or other things, they became bloody, and injuries were not uncommon.

The males and females had distinctive functions, but so-called women's work was valued on the same level as men's work (at least until contact with the Europeans changed the economy of the towns). Women were in the domestic sphere, and the men were hunters and warriors. Because of this division, the men dealt with the outside world, but beloved women were occasionally tasked with politics.

When the Europeans first came, the Indians primarily dealt with traders. They traded slaves (usually from the Florida area) and deerskins and, especially in the first years of settlement, food. Soon, the Florida Native American slave trade was depleted because of the dwindling populations.

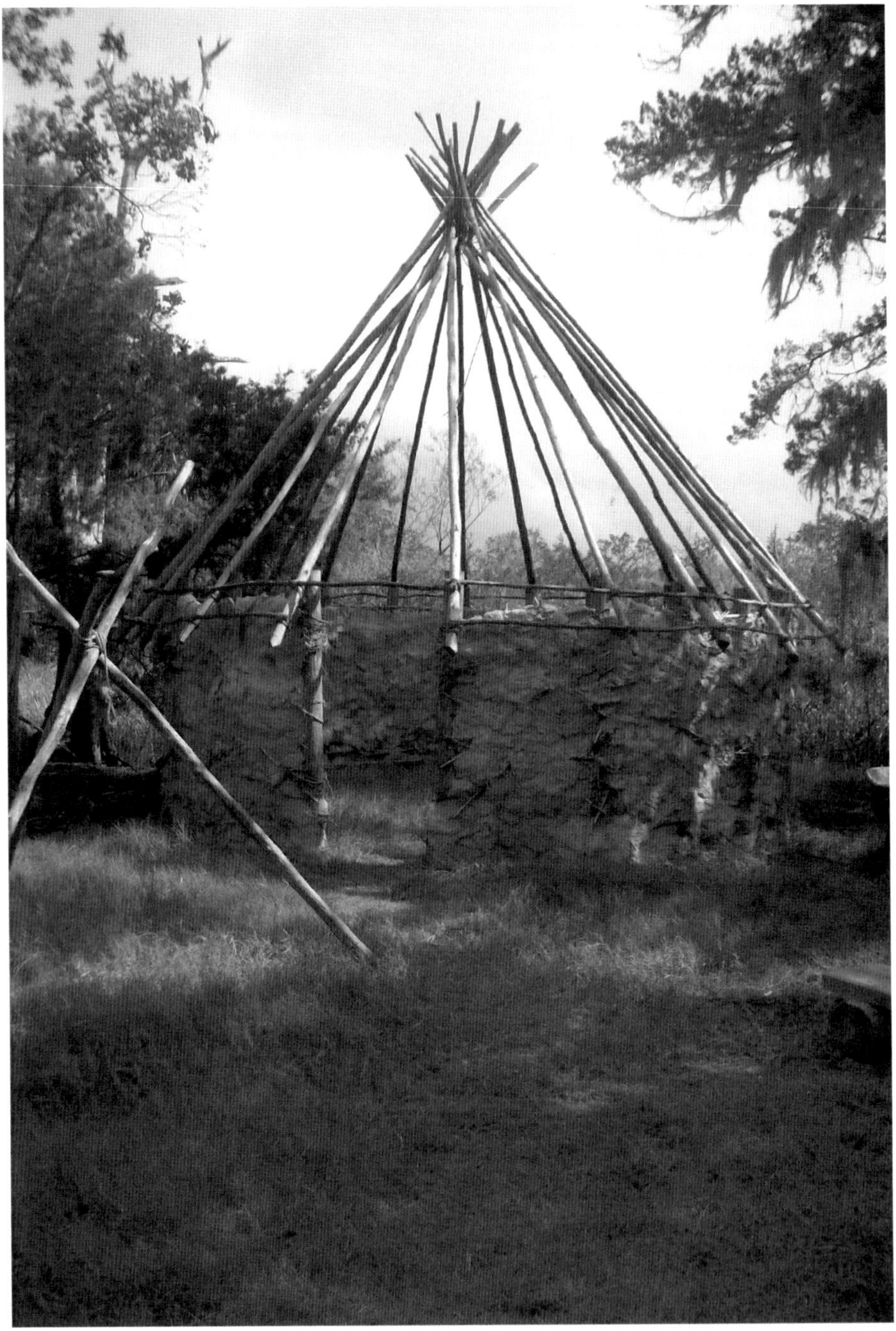

A replica Indian home in progress. *Author's collection.*

As the settlers began to grow their own food, the primary source of trade became deerskins by the early 1800s.

The English, for their convenience, divided the Muskogees into Upper and Lower Creeks. The towns on the Coosa and the Tallapoosa Rivers were known as the Upper Creeks, and those to the southeast on the Chattahoochee and Flint Rivers were the Lower Creeks. The distinction was purely geographical. Because the lower towns were closer to the European settlements of Savannah and Charleston, they were affected more by the contact with these cities. Intermarriage was not uncommon; in fact, for the traders nearest to the Creeks, it was thought a successful survival technique. The upper towns remained less affected by European influences, and they were more traditional in politics and social institutions.

It was the contact with the Europeans and their effect on the economies of the Creeks that brought social change in the tribes. The Europeans' excessive need for more and more land pushed the Creeks out of Georgia and eventually led to their forced removal to Oklahoma.

6

TOMOCHICHI, A FOUNDER OF GEORGIA

Tomochichi was one of the great men of Georgia history. His gentle acceptance of the inevitability of the presence of the colonists helped the Creeks survive and live in peace for over three decades. The Creeks were eventually forced out from Georgia, but Tomochichi delayed the inevitable in his lifetime. Tomochichi and Oglethorpe's friendship and working relationship facilitated a peaceful beginning to Georgia.

Tomochichi was probably born of a Yamasee father and Creek mother. It was not unusual for different tribal members to marry in the land of Georgia. The Creeks were a loose confederation with fluid tribal connections. The Yamasees were not part of the confederation, but they often allied with the Creeks in common causes. Tomochichi was a product of this culture. He was proud of his heritage and fought to preserve it against the onslaught of European settlement. Paradoxically, he worked to create a symbiosis of the Creek and English cultures. He was a practical idealist in a time of massive change and challenge for the Creek people.

Tomochichi married Senauki, a strong woman, who proved to be an invaluable partner. She was by his side during most of the major events in his life. The Creeks were a matrilineal society, meaning they transferred their power and lineage through the woman. Tomochichi and Senauki, for some reason, appear to never have had children. This led Tomochichi to choose Toonahowi, his nephew through Senauki, as his heir apparent.

Tomochichi, early in life, had established himself as a strong soldier. Ouekachumpa of the Ocona Creeks called him a "great warrior." Another

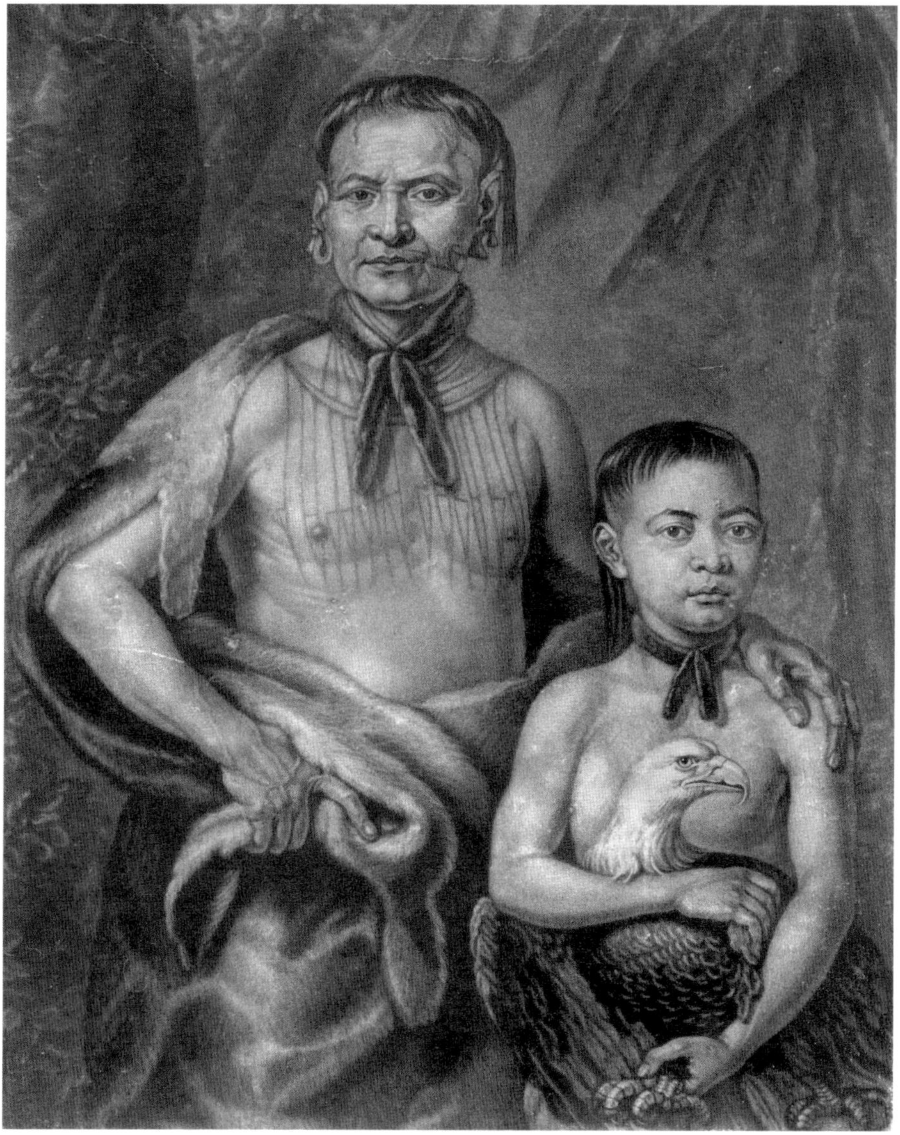

A print by John Faber of William Verelst's (1704–1752) painting of Tomochichi and Toonahowi. *Courtesy of Telfair Museums.*

proof of this was the amount of slaves he traded. Slaves were usually obtained through battle with other Indian tribes. The British wrote that he was unscrupulous in his business. These words were probably no more than proof he achieved fair deals for himself and his tribe and was not as easily taken advantage of as some of the other Indians. Tomochichi appears to have been against the ill-fated Yamasee War in 1715. He probably did not assist with the war against the English because he was comfortable with his trade arrangements. Also, the Lower Creeks did not, as a rule, participate in the war. He more than likely foresaw the ultimate result of the battle and felt the best way forward was to try to navigate a way with the English and not against them. When the war ended, the Creeks signed a treaty with the British but not the Cherokees because of the other Indians' treachery in the war. The war with the Cherokees continued for another twenty years. When the treaty with the English was signed and the territory realigned, Tomochichi's village was left out of the new boundaries of the Creek Nation. He was essentially a man without a country. Why had the Creeks done this? Slave-trading fellow Indians did not earn him friends, and although most, if not all, villages participated in the slave trade, Tomochichi was apparently exceptional at this practice. Also, his interests were not of concern to the Creeks who had gone to war. After all, he sat on the sidelines, content to watch while they did battle. He also did not seem to participate in the new war with the Cherokees, which was precipitated by their siding with the British during the Yamasee War. Because he was not a participant in either of these conflicts, he was not a member in good standing with the Creeks. Finally, his village was on the edge of Creek territory and probably sometimes held dual alliances with Spain and the British. Siding with Spanish mission Indians at times and with the Creeks at others likely made him a dubious, at best, character in the Creek Nation.

So Tomochichi was without a people. Many members of his village left to join other villages for protection. He was abandoned, as both the Creeks and the English did not support his or any other Creek presence there. He probably did not want to join another tribe as a member and not as the mico. He did not believe the attitudes that the Creeks had toward the British settlers promised much of a future. This left him in a grave crisis. He was in his sixties; what would he do? There must have been enormous emotional and spiritual pain, as everything he knew seemed to disappear overnight. There also was ever-present physical danger. Living alone with his family left him vulnerable to attack from other tribes and the British. This must have been a period of deep soul-searching for the once confident leader. Was there a path through this and, if so, where?

Tomochichi's next move was bold, especially considering his age and the turmoil in the world around him. He returned to the abandoned land of his fathers and mothers on the coast. A return to the roots of his heritage would possibly regenerate his life. This dramatic reconnection with his Creek heritage showed his devotion to that heritage. It also made Tomochichi, the alienated exile, the keeper of the heritage—a challenge to those who would disparage him or cast him as an outsider. At some point, Tomochichi appears to have pleaded with the British to establish a town in the so-called Debatable Lands. He was present when South Carolina government officials discussed establishing a trading post—near what would later be called Savannah—with John and Mary. At this meeting, it appears that Tomochichi's new tribe was given the blessings of the Carolina government to settle near the Musgrove trading post on the Yamacraw bluff.

He had a new vision that had slowly come from his soul-searching time. The Creeks had to recognize the new world that was fast approaching them. The land he chose was debatable—no one had control of it. It was a place one could settle without competition and not be disturbed. He extended an invitation to Native Americans who wanted to build something a little different. They created a new tribe, the Yamacraws. The tribe cherished the unique power and beauty of their culture. Yet at the same time, this new tribe looked to trade and not war with the English settlers. They also looked to the future by learning to live with the English. This eventually included understanding the language, culture and mores of the British. This new tribe became an example of how to maintain their heritage and work with the British. Tomochichi was through with warring tribes and battles with the settlers. He was through with the slave trade and trading with the British, too often at a loss, for goods that did so much harm to his people, such as alcohol. He had a dream; what was left was the work to make it happen.

Tomochichi chose the bluff above the Savannah River, where the city of Savannah now stands, to start his new tribe. He claimed his ancestors' place connected him to a shared past with the Creeks, despite the current circumstances. It also provided first access to British ships that might land. Therefore, he had the first crack at the traders who came by sea from the Carolinas. It was a treacherous trek over land for the English hazarding struggles with Native Americans and possibly the Spanish, who often made military junkets into what were called the Debatable Lands. He took Senauki, Toonahowi and others with him. The new tribe he gathered consisted of around two hundred Creeks and Yamasees. One can assume that if they had been for the war, they wanted to start something new and were ready to be part of Tomochichi's new vision.

It was for some of these same reasons that Oglethorpe wanted to start the colony on the bluff. He could see the Spanish ships coming into the mainland and protect the land from the Spanish ships. It also had a great natural port, which would be essential to the development of the new colony. The problem was, while the British considered it their land, the Native Americans did not. Oglethorpe's first challenge was to convince the Yamacraws to allow him to peacefully settle on their land.

Tomochichi's meeting with Oglethorpe was problematic, as the Englishman asked this new acquaintance to move and make room for his vision of a colony. Oglethorpe was a strong believer that all men were created equal. He rejected the plantation mentality of the Carolina colonies. Therefore, he treated the mico as an equal and referred to him as a king, recognizing his stature among his people. Of course, calling Tomochichi a king also gave him the right to negotiate treaties with Oglethorpe, which made dealing with the many tribes of the Creek Confederation a little less onerous. Oglethorpe was a man who was intruding in Native American land but respected the native people. Tomochichi surely noticed this. Oglethorpe was an idealist, as was Tomochichi. Tomochichi (in his late eighties) probably looked on the thirty-three-year-old Oglethorpe as a young leader who needed guidance. Oglethorpe, whose father had died when he was young, might have seen a father figure who offered him the keys to the kingdom. Tomochichi may even have seen Oglethorpe as an adopted son.

Oglethorpe's plans for the colony would have brought hope to the elderly mico, as it wouldn't be for the fancy English elite, who thought of themselves as superiors and had insatiable lust for more slaves and land, as in Charleston. One of the major complaints against the Carolina settlers was they often entrapped the Native Americans in debt, causing them to take desperate actions to repay them. Because of the colonists' racist or condescending attitudes toward the Native Americans, this debt often accumulated; the Carolinians allowed English traders to practice unscrupulous deals with the Native Americans without consequences. The plan Oglethorpe laid before Tomochichi was to bring the common worker and tradesman of England to the colony. Oglethorpe planned a city that resonated with the planned mound cities of the Creeks. The colony would not have slaves, which had caused such friction between the English and the Native Americans. The English settlers of South Carolina were always paying Native Americans money for the capture and enslavement of other tribal members. This caused dissension among the tribes, as they kidnapped members of others to sell to the English. The other great troublemaker of English and Indian relationships was the sale and trade of whiskey to the Native Americans. The new colony would outlaw the use of alcohol. Oglethorpe also promised

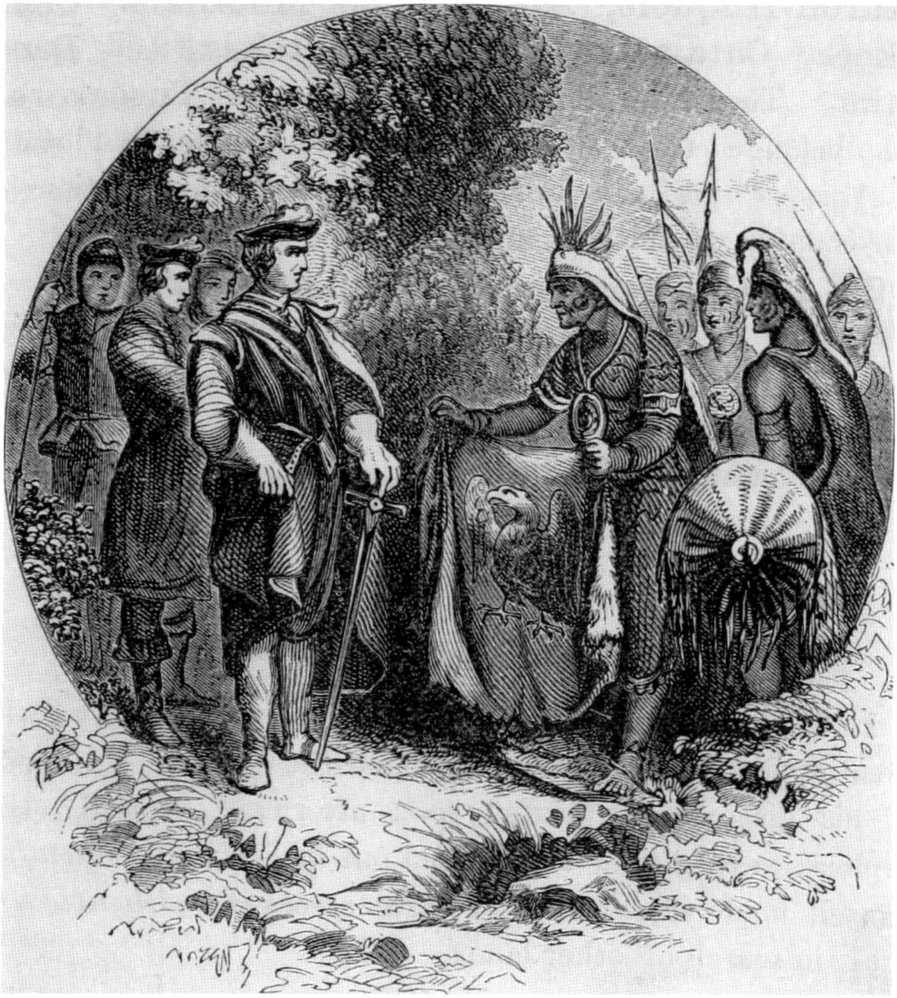

The first meeting of Oglethorpe and Tomochichi, General Oglethorpe meeting the Creek Nation. Print originally published in John Lossing's *An Outline History of the United States* (Sheldon & Company, 1881). *Image uploaded by Flickr user Internet Archive Book Images.*

to bring the n'er-do-well traders under control. Oglethorpe was open to learning from the Native American culture, too, a markedly different attitude from most of the leaders of the other colonies.

Tomochichi was in his later years and did not have the tendencies of a mercurial temperament. He could trust and see Oglethorpe was interested in finding ways that the two worlds could work together. His tribe consisted of members who had not been involved in warring with the British in the

Yamasee War. The Yamacraws were looking to coexist with the British, not challenge them. Tomochichi wanted to learn about (not necessarily to convert to) the Christian religion and encouraged the development of a mission school for his tribe. He even attended a Christian service. This was remarkable openness considering his age. He was also interested in his young protégé Toonahowi learning the English language, culture and politics to better create a bridge between the two worlds. Tomochichi was developing a new model on how to work with the British.

Thus, when Oglethorpe explained he needed the land on which the Yamacraws were currently living to create his new settlement Savannah, Tomochichi was open to hearing this proposal—cautious but not threatened. Tomochichi probably realized that if he gave the land to Oglethorpe, he would no longer have to wait for the British to sail into the bluff for trade. They would have ongoing access to the British who settled in Savannah. Tomochichi believed there was enough land for both. He did not have ships that needed a harbor, as Oglethorpe did. If he moved his tribe a few miles inward, he could have first access and control of the trade and be the natural envoy between the Creeks and the British. Here was a chance to begin, not necessarily a merger, but maybe a confederation with the British.

Tomochichi saw in Oglethorpe a way to strengthen his tenuous relationships with the other Creek tribes. If he became the primary liaison between the Creeks and the British, he could claim a place of prominence among the Creeks. This was as essential for the survival of his tribe as maintaining good terms with the British were. Oglethorpe would become so comfortable with the Creeks he would later exclaim he felt as if he was a Native American. Tomochichi and Oglethorpe would learn, if not to love, then to deeply respect each other.

These two men knew they had found a remarkable opportunity in each other to create something good and new for both their worlds. They also knew that their agreements had to be mutually beneficial. It was fortuitous that they made the deal and continued to develop their relationship.

After the treaty was agreed on, Tomochichi took an interest in assisting Oglethorpe in developing the colony. One of the keys to the survival of Savannah were outposts or forts to defend against the incursions of the Spanish and French. Oglethorpe established Fort King George in Darien on the site of an old Guale village. Tomochichi may have been influential in the selection of the site. We do know that Tomochichi traveled with Oglethorpe to decide the southern border of the Georgia colony.

Tomochichi was instrumental in helping Oglethorpe create the first road in Georgia to Darien along Indian trails. The road was essential to create a supply and communication route to keep the forts and Savannah connected to one another. He assisted with the road to another outpost, later to be called Augusta. Tomochichi was helpful in the disputes that constantly arose between the Indians and the settlers. He promoted Oglethorpe among the Creeks as an Englishman they could work with. For his part, Tomochichi stated he was impressed with the Christian message of love, but he was not impressed enough to adopt the Christian religion. He was open to learning English ways but remained sure of his Creek identity.

In late 1733, Oglethorpe was under attack for what the trustees considered his neglect of reports about the colony. The trustees, in order to correct this problem, requested that Oglethorpe return to England and explain the progress of the colony. Oglethorpe, who had been busy bringing the colony to fruition, knew he needed unique evidence of what he had been doing. One of his greatest achievements thus far had been the coalition-building he had done with the Native Americans. Unlike the other colonies, especially South Carolina, he had developed a healthy relationship with the Indians in the Georgia colony. This had assisted in the security of the settlement. The Native Americans did not attack them and assisted with keeping the Spanish in Florida. But these relationships were not self-evident, so he invited Tomochichi and other Indian leaders to go with him to show the trustees he had made good inroads with the Native Americans. The question, was, would Tomochichi be open to travel to England? After all, Tomochichi was older and may not have felt any need to go. But Tomochichi accepted because he saw it would offer him and his people (now he was representative of the Creeks too) great benefit.

Tomochichi probably considered it would be good to develop direct relationships with the English power structure so that the Creeks would not have to use a white intermediary in their treaty and trade talks. He also knew that this trip would increase his stature among the Creeks and ensure the Yamacraws' growing partnership with the Creek Nation. As the Indians nearest to the British, the Yamacraws' ongoing contact with the British needed to enhance their relationship. Building relationships overseas with the British could increase the power of the tribe. Tomochichi, being older, also saw an opportunity for Toonahowi to come with him and learn more about the British and create personal alliances, which could aid the Yamacraws and Creeks when he replaced Tomochichi. Last, but probably not least, it would help his friend and alliance partner Oglethorpe.

The trustees wanted Oglethorpe to make a personal report on the status of the colony. He had not been in good communication with the trustees because he was too busy settling the newly arrived Salzburgers. (He had to arrange land for their settlement from the Creeks and ensure they were able to make a good start of their new town, New Ebenezer.) To Oglethorpe's delight, the Salzburgers were an industrious people and were doing well. The settlement was running smoothly, and the Yamacraws were adjusting to them well. All of this activity left no time for communication with the trustees. He may have used all of this as an excuse to keep the trustees from interfering with his work. But he could no longer keep them in the dark.

The trustees were interested in meeting with Tomochichi. They wanted to impress the Native Americans with their vast power and, in their view, superior culture. They were convinced that an impressive display would ensure the Native Americans' compliance with the colonies' treaties and even tilt the various treaties in their favor. Yet they also knew the Creeks were crucial in the security of the young colony. The Creeks helped in cutting the cost for troops required to protect the colonies, which in a struggling economy was a valuable asset to have. So the adventure was on, and they left for Charleston on March 23, 1734. There they waited a few weeks for their ship to England.

Upon their arrival in London, the Creek representatives began their mission of diplomacy. The trustees paid for English-style clothes for the Creeks to prevent people from gawking as much and not offend English sensibilities. The Creek chiefs did not wear these clothes in the formal meetings, and they surely were a little taken aback by the request. Tomochichi, who as chief representative and king, expected to dress in his native garb, but Senauki and Toonahowi dressed in the English manner. The English were not to be scandalized by their customary sparse clothing, which showed so much of their skin. They wore the clothes, but they did not abandon their tribal face paintings or hairstyles, keeping a visible remnant of their culture. The British, for their part, put the Native Americans in impressive lodgings and transported them around in royal carriages. They were determined to show the grandeur of Britain.

On the third of July, the first diplomatic meeting with the trustees took place. Tomochichi, for the first time, acted as the representative of the Creeks without an intermediary. The Creeks pleaded their case for themselves. Through the translator, John Musgrove, Tomochichi, apologetic for this need, made his first introduction. He made one of his primary requests for his people to be trained in the Christian and English ways so that they

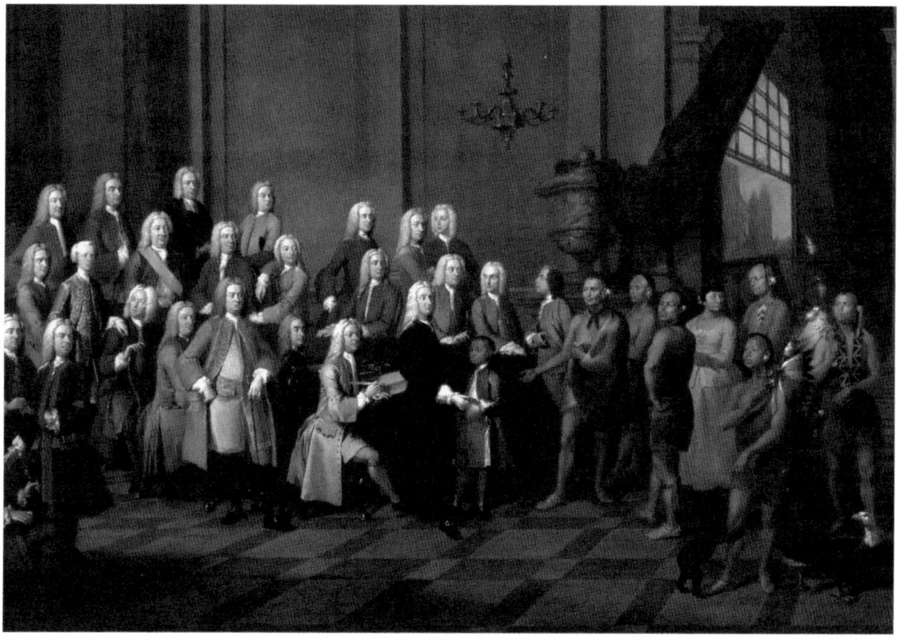

Painting by William Verelst of Tomochichi and other Creeks in meeting with the Georgia Trustees (notice Senauki in the dress of an English woman). *Wikimedia Commons.*

could be better partners. Of course, it would also eliminate the need for interpreters or intermediaries in their negotiations with the British. He expressed his desire to complete the bonding of the two peoples before he died. He thanked Oglethorpe for his friendship and his fair treatment of the Indians, taking care that Oglethorpe was seen as crucial to the bond with the British. He continued, using language from his culture about the Great One Above and the Great Spirit, thanking the spirit for safe travels and for preserving him from his enemies, which resonated with the Christian British. He was acting as ambassador par excellence. The British could not help but be impressed with his presence and language. The meeting was seen as historic and the beginning of a long term of peace between the two nations. As such, the British commissioned a painter, William Verelst, to depict the scene. It was widely reported by the British press, as were all of the events surrounding the Creeks' time in England.

In August, Tomochichi was treated to a visit with the king and queen at Kensington Palace. Again, he displayed his diplomatic skills, stating, "I am come for the good of the children of the Nations of the Upper and Lower Creeks that they may be instructed in the knowledge of the English." Much like the passing of the Olympic torch, he presented them with eagle feathers that had been carried from town to town as a symbol of peace to the Creeks. Tomochichi, through the symbolism of children and eagles, had presented common ground with the king and queen. Who could deny children a blessing and protection? Tomochichi pressed for fair trade relations and the education of his people. He advocated for these two greatest treaty desires wherever he found himself.

Tomochichi was taken for a carriage ride to see the vast estate of Kensington Palace and was awed, but he also observed, "The English men knew many things his countrymen did not, but doubted if they were happier, since we live worse than them and they more innocently [simply]." Tomochichi came from a culture that did not respect the accumulation of goods for personal sake and showed some bewilderment that the British constantly wanted more.

Slowly, the Creeks were winning the respect of the British nation. They did not affect English pretentions but were straightforward in their talk and manners. They appeared civilized enough and nonthreatening; thus, it was being generally assumed they could be dealt with as partners (although, of course, as junior partners).

The stay continued; Tomochichi met the Archbishop of Canterbury and Archbishop William Wake at Lambeth Palace. Tomochichi always made his plea for the Christian teaching of his people. Yet when the archbishops or others asked to discuss their religious beliefs with the Creeks, they claimed it was taboo to talk of such things in normal conversations. This may have been yet another diplomatic way of avoiding controversial subjects when they arose. The Earl of Egmont, a powerful trustee, even commented about the cultural accommodations they made to advance their own agenda. Apparently, the Native Americans had no trouble discussing their religion with him, as he noted how their two views of God were similar and might pave the way to their conversion. The Creeks apparently were comfortable with the earl's open mind.

In time, the trustees selected Oglethorpe and two other trustees to discuss what was needed for a treaty of land and peace to be accepted by the Creeks. Tomochichi asked that their children be taught Christianity and that a fair regulation of trade be made between the Native Americans and colonists. He requested that a fair weight system be adopted and rum not be sold. He also listed British goods that the Native Americans wanted access to. He also requested what we would call a favored nation agreement. The Creeks, especially the Yamacraws, wanted to receive better trade prices than other Native Americans. While no agreement was signed, the trustees began to work in their government and with the merchants and traders, seeking a standardization of prices with the Creeks.

Other chiefs made various personal requests. Notably, Toonahowi asked for guns for the men of his tribe. To seal the deal, he recited the Lord's Prayer and Apostles' Creed and read from a random English book lying on the table. One cannot help but see Tomochichi's wry smile as he watched his young protégé at work.

It was time for the Creeks to return home. The English felt they had impressed the Native Americans with their pomp and circumstance and the great buildings and knew they would not have any trouble with these Creeks. They were allies to the colonists' cause. Tomochichi's question to a trustee showed he might be an ally, but his eyes were wide open: "Why did the English go out of a land of such plenty to seek support in a foreign country?" This observation demonstrated his awareness of the imperialistic nature of the British Empire.

When Tomochichi arrived home, he continued to entwine the two cultures as well as could be expected. In 1736, a Christian school opened at the Irene Mounds for his people. He asked John Wesley, the Anglican minister, to start a school, but Wesley had demurred. Tomochichi even asked the king of England, but nothing had happened. At last, Wesley assigned the Moravian minister Ingham. Tomochichi was not looking for his tribe to become Christians. The school taught Christianity in addition to reading and writing English. This prevented future problems dealing with traders and treaties that they did not fully understand. They began to be clued into the mores of the white men. This, too, better prepared them for the onslaught of settlers and the never-ending quest for the British to spread their empire.

Tomochichi also worked with Oglethorpe in securing the southern border of Georgia, which he had been influential in delineating. This border was not only protected by the Yamacraw and the rest of the Creeks but also by the settlers, who would be by their side against Floridian Indians and Spanish intrusions. He had shown Oglethorpe old Indian trails that led to the southern Fort of King George in Darien and Fort Frederica in St. Simons. The roads were used daily by colonists and Creeks alike. These roads ensured that the capable Spanish fleets could not cut off communication and supply routes.

In 1739, Tomochichi was about to accomplish the grand goal of leading the Creeks in signing a treaty cementing the British and Creeks relationship. Oglethorpe was to travel with Tomochichi to the great Creek city of

Coweta, where representatives of the tribes of the confederation, Choctaws and Chickasaw were to be present. It was to be the climax of the work he and Oglethorpe had strived for these many years of their relationship. Unfortunately, Tomochichi was unable to travel with Oglethorpe. The great man was dying. He could not witness the event.

Toonahowi, his adopted nephew, did not go either, remaining at Tomochichi's bedside. Senauki, his wife, was there too, as was his tribe, waiting outside of his home as a show of support. Tomochichi knew that he had trained Toonahowi in the ways of a mico and in the ways of the English. Toonahowi had the tools to continue bridging the gap between the two ways. He had the added bonus of youth, whereas Tomochichi was in his last years when he met Oglethorpe; Toonahowi was young and had a long life to build on this legacy with Oglethorpe and the rest of the settlers. He was leaving his tribe, between Toonahowi and Senauki, in capable hands.

So as Tomochichi came to the end of his life, the consolidation of the two proud heritages seemed inevitable. He was leaving his new tribe and the Creek Confederation in good stead to build a new way with these Georgian settlers. He had achieved the utopia he had once seen possible in the eyes and ways of Oglethorpe.

Oglethorpe, upon Tomochichi's death, wanted to give him an English burial to emphasize to the settlers his significance in the settling of Georgia. Oglethorpe and Tomochichi appeared to have agreed to his final resting place. Otherwise, it would be unlikely that the Yamacraws would have allowed him to bury their leader in such a manner and place. In the words of William Stephens, a British soldier and a pallbearer at the ceremony, recorded in his journal:

> [T]*he most material Thing which happened abroad, and I thought worth notig* [sic], *was the Death of the old Mico Thomo Chichi, said to be upwards of ninety Years of Age: And as the General always esteemed him a Friend of the Colony, and therefore showed him particular Marks of his Esteem, when living; so he distinguished him at his Death, ordering his Corpse to be brought down; and it was buried in the Centre of one of the principal Squares, the General being pleased to make himself one of his Pall-Bearers, with five others, among whom he laid his Commands on me to be one, and the other four were military Officers: At the Depositing of the Corpse, seven Minute Guns were fired, and about forty Men in Arms (as many as could instantly be found) gave three Vollies over the Grave; which the General says he intends to dignify with some Obelisk, or the like,*

> *over it, as an Ornament to the Town, and a Memorial to the Indians, how great Regard the English would pay to all their Nations, who maintain true Friendship with us.*

The placement of Tomochichi's grave in a square in the center of town was to symbolically show the English and the Native Americans alike that they were a united people. The fact that Oglethorpe gave him the formal burial ceremony of an English dignitary further cemented this symbolism. Tomochichi had literally been made a part of the landscape of the city. It was an eternal reminder of his gentle spirit, which had allowed a peaceful settlement of Georgia and of the welcoming and cooperative spirits the two peoples shared.

Unfortunately, one can only take responsibility for one's time on earth. You can open the door to possibilities, but your influence wanes from the moment you pass from this earth. The legacy you create is left to be rejected or accepted by the next generation. But Tomochichi's protégé Toonahowi took up the challenging mantle. It was time for him to show what kind of leader he would be.

7

TOONAHOWI, FOREVER YOUNG

Toonahowi was to become the embodiment of the broken dreams of his forefathers and mothers. He was the heir to the chiefdom of the Yamacraws. But in colonial Native American life, while leaders may have had the familial right, they also needed to show merit. Most scholars say Toonahowi was the nephew of Tomochichi through the matrilineal line of Senauki. He was called this often during his lifetime. But some say, in reality, he was Senauki's grandson from her first marriage. He was born sometime in the early 1720s and spent most of his life living with the Yamacraws.

He grew up in the shadow of the Yamasee War. There was a general disillusionment with the war and a wonder what war with the British could accomplish. This conflict had shown the Creeks the need to unite. But it also demonstrated the need to learn to live with the British or potentially see their culture disappear. While being a good warrior was a grand vision for every Creek boy, it was now necessary more than ever to learn to be a diplomat.

He was trained in the ways of a Creek boy. He learned to track and hunt. He also learned to play chunkey and a stickball game very much like lacrosse. He was often by Tomochichi's side so that he could learn how to be a good mico. His training was like that of every other future mico—that is, until a ship with Oglethorpe and his scouting team sailed up the Savannah River. His training included the ins and outs of Creek life, but he had to master the English way of life, too.

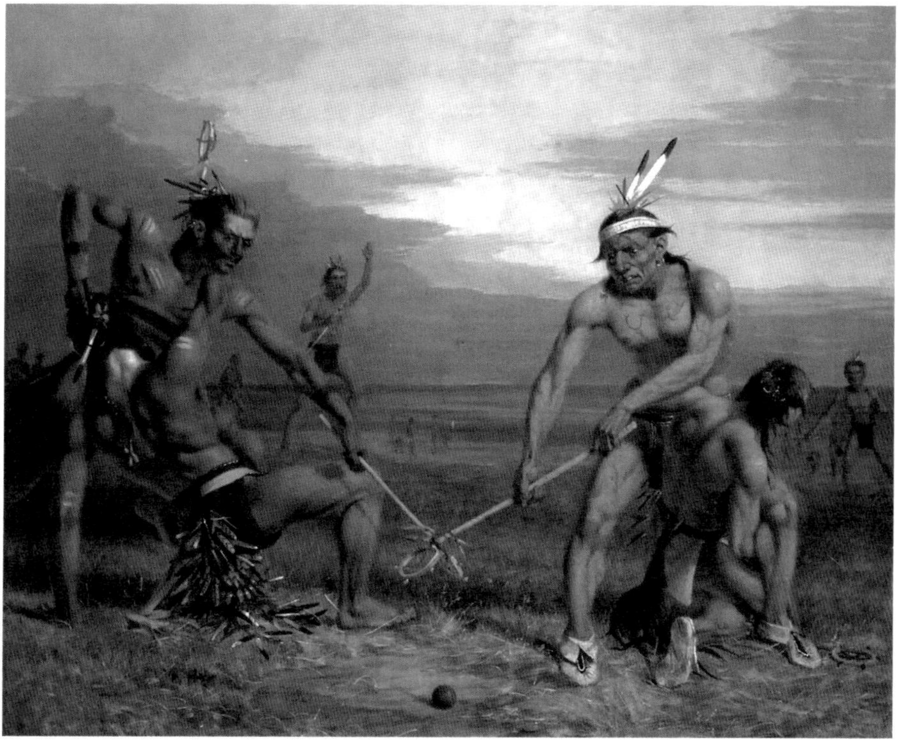

A physical Indian stickball game. Charles Deas (1818–1867). *Public domain.*

At an early age, he was trained to speak English by Mary Musgrove. He attended Christian services and learned about the Bible. He received an English education and ate at table with the British.

Because Tomochchi was old and wise, he felt the need to ensure that Toonahowi's education was of the best quality. He spent more time than usual with the boy, but Toonahowi was a quick learner. In three months' time, he developed a reasonably good grasp of English letters and figures.

In 1734, twelve-year-old Toonahowi joined Tomochichi, Senauki and seven other Creeks on a voyage that a Creek boy could only imagine. He crossed the Atlantic Ocean to travel to England. But it was not all adventure; three times a week, he studied with Samuel Smith, an Anglican minister and trustee of the colony. He learned to recite the Lord's Prayer and the Ten Commandments. He traveled with the Creek party as they visited various famous people and places. The Earl of Egmont noted that he read with a good accent. Toonahowi's presence on the trip reminded the British that the Creeks were indeed interested in learning the English ways and living peacefully with them.

The highlight of the visit was an audience with King George II and Queen Caroline. The queen stroked Toonahowi's face and offered him presents. A month later, he showed a unique emotional intelligence, as he now knew how to obtain what he wanted from the English. He asked the Georgia Trustees for guns for his brothers at home, and to earn this, he recited the Lord's Prayer and the Apostles' Creed. The distribution of guns to his friends and future braves would help build a bond and allegiance to him. So the young and future mico was already learning how to lead.

In October, toward the last of the trip, Prince William, the Duke of Cumberland, presented a gold pocket watch to Toonahowi. Toonahowi accepted and told everyone the correct time. The watch became a prize possession of his and appeared to bring back pleasant memories of this trip to England. In all his actions, although he was often treated more as a novelty than a child, he demonstrated a demeanor that gave confidence to the British that they could be partners with the Creek people.

During his trip in England, he was in two paintings. One painting was of the trustees and the Creeks. Tomochichi was dressed in Creek attire and shown as the leader. Interestingly enough, in between the Creeks and the trustees stands Toonahowi, dressed as an English boy. One can only suppose that he was demonstrating his ability to be British or, as the British would have thought, civilized. He represented the future—the Creeks were capable of being British. The second painting is of him and Tomochichi in full Creek attire. Tomochichi has his hand on Toonahowi, and the boy is holding an eagle, a sign of peace to the Creeks. This was a subtle message that Toonahowi s generation sought to bring peace. In both paintings, Toonahowi is used as a metaphor for the hopes between the Creeks and British.

In October 1734, the Creeks returned to Georgia. Toonahowi stood as one of the Creeks who had met the British in their land. This, in Creek eyes, lifted his status in the world. Tomochichi included Toonahowi in his meetings and discussions of the Indians' diplomatic endeavors. Toonahowi, though young, was becoming more influential in Yamacraw and Creek life.

In June, Chigelley, the mico of Coweta, after hearing about the adventures and diplomacy of the English trip, declared that Senauki was the mother, Tomochichi the father and Toonahowi the chief ruler of them all in his stead. Chigelley concluded with a blessing that Toonahowi would be a great man and bring good things to himself and the Creek people.

Tomochichi and the Yamacraws's relationship with the rest of the Creeks was fully restored. But more importantly, Toonahowi was publicly affirmed as the mico-in-waiting for the Yamacraws and held a distinguished position in the Creek Nation as a whole.

Toonahowi was present when the Yamacraws met with John Wesley for the first time. Wesley was to fulfill Tomochichi's long requested training of Indian children in Christian ways. Toonahowi never attended the schools because of his age. He was a teenager and had previous training while in England and by the Musgroves. Instead, he traveled with Tomochichi, Oglethorpe and other members of the military entourage to delineate what should be the southern border of Georgia. Toonahowi was now of an age to act as Tomochichi's second and mico-in-training. Although Toonahowi was the chosen successor, he still had to prove that he had the warrior skills necessary to lead the Yamacraw tribe. Instead of wearing English clothes for diplomatic purposes, he had to wear the warrior and tribal garb of a Creek. He mastered the ability to know whether he was to appear as an English gentleman or Creek warrior.

On this trip, in the spring of 1736, as they traveled the newly defined Georgia border, they named the various barrier islands of Georgia. Toonahowi insisted that one of the islands be named Cumberland Island for the duke who had given him the gold watch in England. Slowly, Toonahowi was becoming more influential, and he was already showing some diplomatic skills.

After this trip, Tomochichi had bouts of illnesses and probably became more and more dependent on Toonahowi to share the leadership of the Yamacraws. We know that Toonahowi did not travel to the meeting of Oglethorpe and the Creek leadership at Coweta, as he stayed by the ailing Tomochichi's side in August 1739. This meeting resulted in the Treaty of Coweta. This shows the young Toonahowi was loyal to his adopted father and more interested in his well-being than in garnering more prestige in the Creek community. Tomochichi died two months later, in October.

The death of Tomochichi had to have been a transformational time for Toonahowi. He was now mico. How would he lead? His first challenge was the British declaration of war with Spain that led to the international War of Jenkin's Ear. It appears Toonahowi was concerned as much as Oglethorpe was to assert the boundaries of Georgia and once and for all vanquish the Spanish from the land. If the Yamacraw were to align themselves with the British, the safety of his tribe rested with the English holding their territorial integrity. So it is no surprise that we next hear of

Toonahowi in southern Georgia with Yamacraw braves. He was scouting and recruiting warriors across the Southeast for the British. Undoubtedly, he was keeping Oglethorpe informed of the whereabouts and actions of the French, Spanish and other tribes. He was building networks; as needed, the British could call upon various towns for Indians to fight against the Spanish, their biggest threat.

As an up-and-coming mico, he needed to solidify his position with the Yamacraws. By this point, no one could question his ability to work as a diplomat with the British or his blood ties with the former mico. One question remained: would he distinguish himself in battle? He had to continue to develop the fragile renewed relationships that the Yamacraws had with the other Creek tribes as well.

Oglethorpe, in light of the declared war, decided to act before the Spanish. He began exploratory raids in Florida to investigate the lay of the land. In a report, Oglethorpe mentioned that Toonahowi and his two hundred braves went on frequent raids in this endeavor. Finally, with a British fleet, his military, Toonahowi's Yamacraws and other Native Americans, some recruited by Toonahowi, Oglethorpe marched south to lay siege to St. Augustine in the summer of 1740. The assault of St. Augustine was a failure, and the slaughter of troops holding Fort Mose hurt Oglethorpe's reputation, as the Spanish fully repelled the British from Florida. Oglethorpe had to wait for the retaliatory attack of the Spanish on Georgia.

After the British waited expectedly, the Spanish finally attacked almost two years later, in July 1742. It was here that Toonahowi acquitted himself as a warrior. When the Spanish landed on St. Simons Island, Oglethorpe sent out Toonahowi and his braves to do reconnaissance. After he understood what he was against, Oglethorpe gathered all the troops he could muster and attacked the Spanish twice. In one of these battles, Toonahowi was described as being fierce, demonstrating his bravery and warrior skills. As he led a charge, he was shot in his right arm by a Spanish officer. He continued the assault forward, reaching across his body to use his left hand to draw a pistol and shoot the officer. This skirmish, called the Battle of Bloody Marsh, was the last full-on attack of the Spanish on Georgia soil.

In September 1743, Oglethorpe returned to England, never to come back. Toonahowi, meanwhile, remained to have minor skirmishes to keep the Spanish in Florida. Toonahowi had proven himself in battle and was ready to fulfill the role for which he had spent a lifetime training. But the fortunes of the Yamacraws died in February 1744 when Toonahowi was killed in a firefight. A bullet struck him in the chest, ending his life.

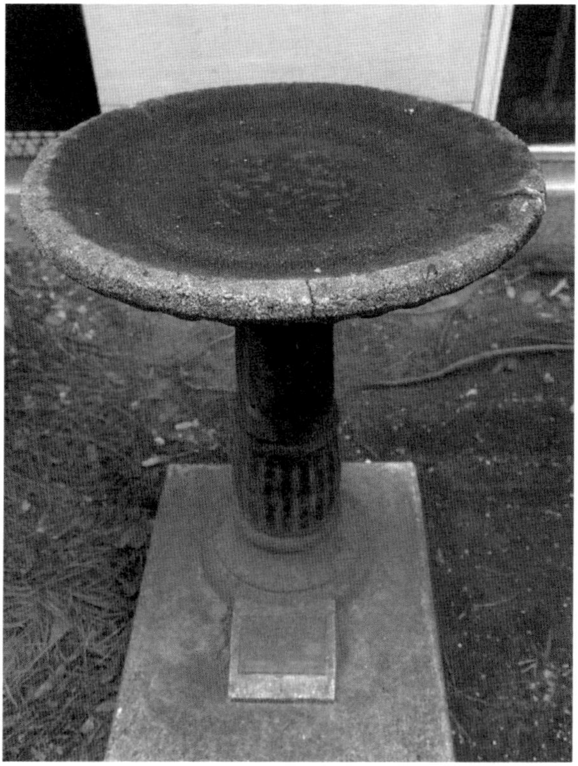

Left: Toonahowi Birdbath. *Author's collection.*

Below: Plaque on Toonahowi Birdbath. *Author's collection.*

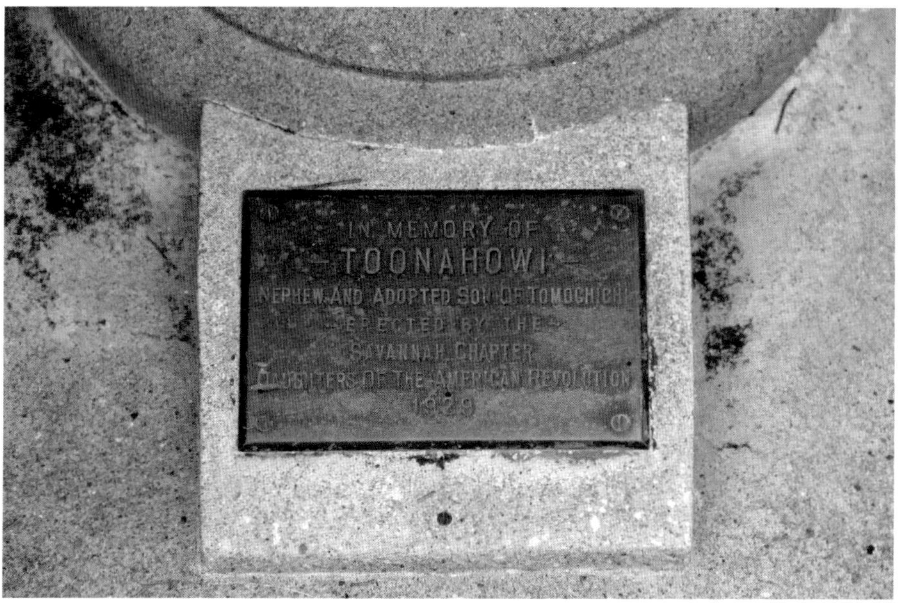

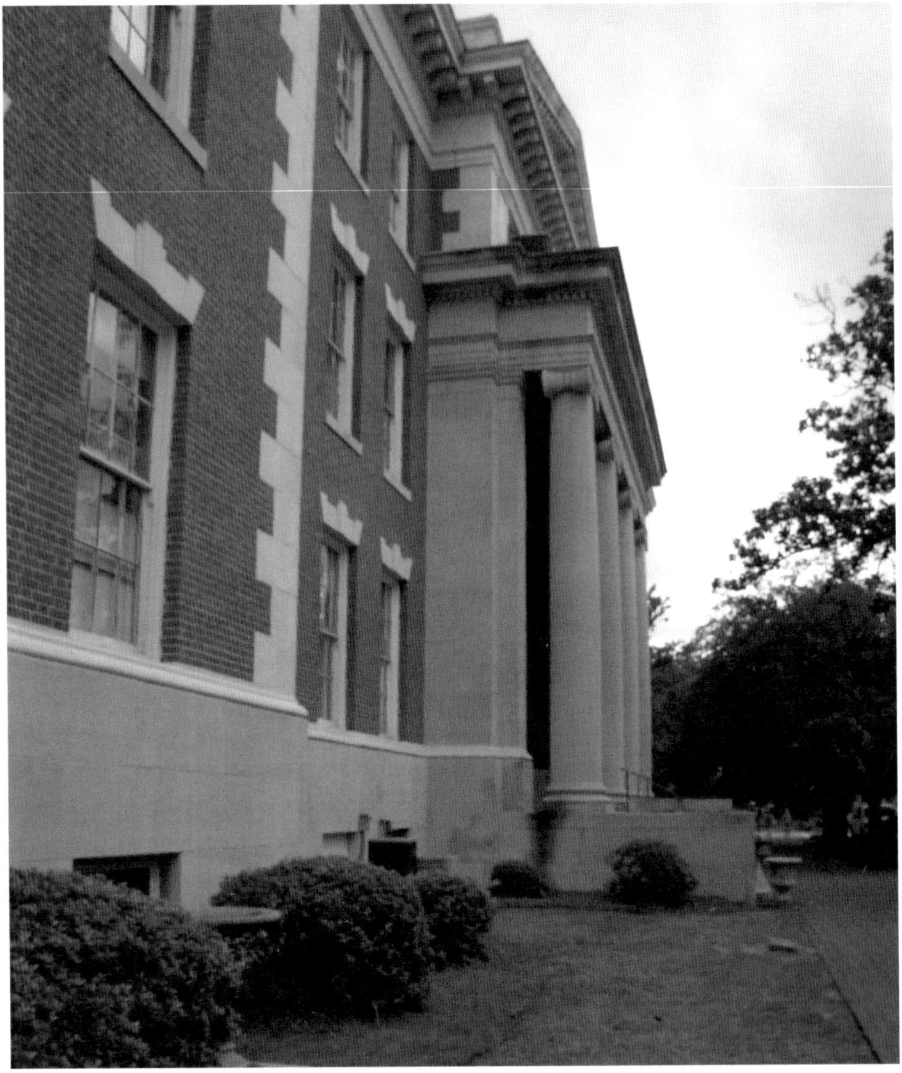

Side view of the board of education building with its birdbath in honor of Toonahowi. *Author's collection.*

Toonahowi was dead in his early twenties. The hopes of Tomochichi and the Yamacraws came to an end.

Toonahowi's body was taken to Cumberland Island, and he was buried there. The island he had named in honor of his English friend became his final resting place. The Yamacraws slowly dispersed and joined the ranks of other Creeks. A dream ended.

8

MALATCHI, BORN TO RULE

Malatchi's father was the legendary Brim, arguably the greatest leader the Creeks ever had. He was the mico of Coweta. This town was solidified as the "head" town of the Lower Creeks and located near Columbus, Georgia, on the Alabama and Georgia state line. Today, Columbus is the county seat of an appropriately named Muscogee County. As was usual for Creeks, Coweta was situated on the Chatahoochee River. It was Mico Brim who, during the Yamasee War in 1715 and for the decade after, guided the Creeks in a stance of neutrality. Some of the Creeks participated in the Yamasee War, and although they lost, they wanted to carry on the conflict with the British. Brim's forceful leadership and vision led the Creeks away from warfare with the British. He envisioned a stronger Creek confederation and, instead of war, diplomacy. He declared for the Creeks a stance of neutrality between the various European powers. He used a diplomatic strategy of pitting the European nations of France, Spain and England against one another. The Europeans, in their efforts to build political and economic ties with the Creeks, were vulnerable. They all desired to have the Creeks on their side and would do most anything to win their allegiance. Brim, during his time as the mico, masterfully worked the Europeans to accomplish the Creeks' goals. His success made him a legend in both the Creek and European worlds.

Malatchi had the fortune and misfortune of being born to such a great father. It would be his fortune to be born into a family whose name commanded respect. It was his misfortune to always be measured by the

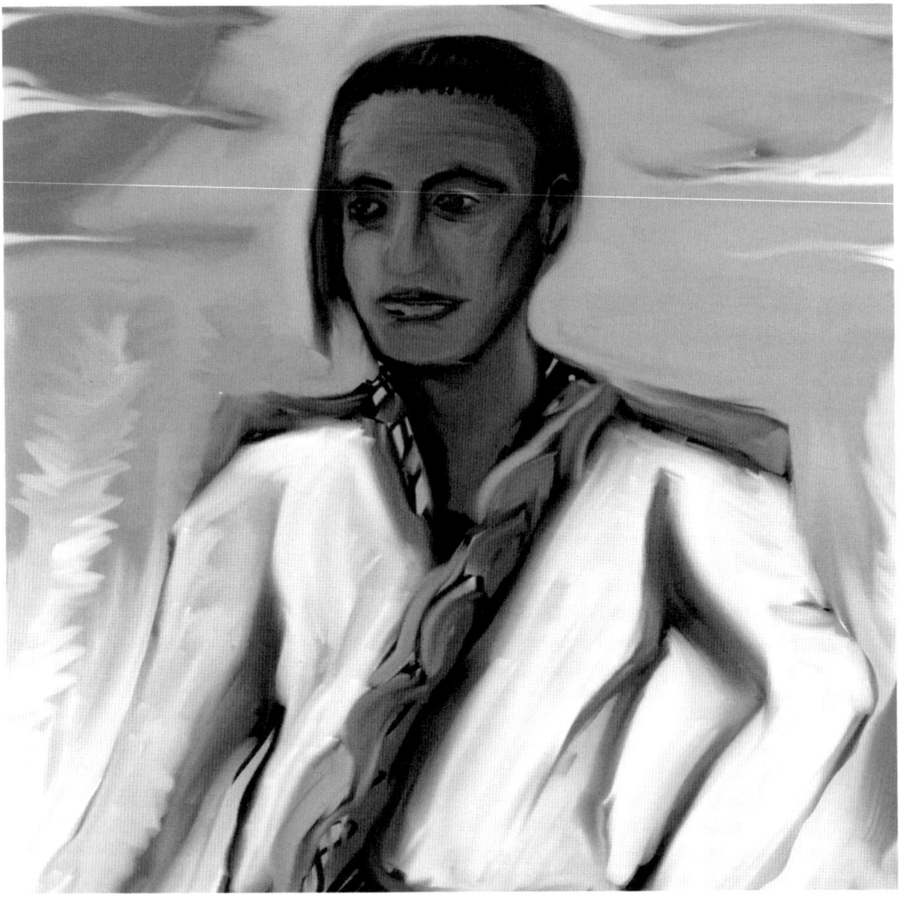

Painting of Malatchi. *Art of Philip Freeman.*

great Brim, his father. It was certain that the son of such a great man would be given his chance to rule, but sometimes, the expectations were greater for him than for other leaders. After all, he was the son of the great Brim. To complicate matters further, he was not the only male heir to the chiefdom. He had a twin brother, Essabo. So not only did he have a father to live up to, he had a brother to whom he would be compared throughout his life as well.

When Brim died, Malatchi and Essabo were too young to claim the chiefdom. They were each given stand-ins to mentor and rule while they came of age: Chigelley for Malatchi and Youhowlakee for Essabo. It is not certain why, but Youhowlakee and Essabo took more prominent leadership roles with the Creeks. So Malatchi became the second in line for the chiefdom. Youhowlakee was in charge until his death in either 1733 or 1734. At his death, Essabo assumed leadership until he died unexpectedly in 1735.

Now one might think that by this time, Malatchi would be ready to rule. But instead, Chigelley took the chiefdom, leaving Malatchi again as the chief-in-waiting. Malatchi eventually bristled at having to wait to take the full chiefdom. But for now, Chigelley and Malatchi's first act was to travel to Savannah for a peace treaty in 1735. Malatchi would be the chief in the early days of the settling of the colony, and Chigelley and he were keen to make friends with the British. Presumably, Tomochichi and Mary Musgrove spoke highly of Oglethorpe, and most of the Indians agreed that the British colonists had more desirable goods. Of course, as previously stated, the Creeks strategically kept a back channel open to the French. This trip was successful for both sides, British and Native American.

Malatchi's trip was the first of many trips to Savannah on behalf of the Creeks. In 1736, he brought Chickasaws and Choctows for the English to meet; they formed an alliance and began to trade with the British. Of course, the head chief, Chigelley, accompanied him on most, if not all, the trips. It should be noted that both Chigelley and Malatchi observed the school that Tomochichi and Wesley established to give an English education to the Yamacraw children. They both appeared to approve. However, they were probably a little more skeptical than Tomochichi had been in regards to where it would lead. Chigelley observed, "Whites knew more than Indians but built big houses as if they were to live forever."

Chigelley did not relinquish power to Malatchi until after he died in 1746. Malatchi was twenty-six. At this time, the Creek Nation, or at least the Lower Creeks, gave him power to speak on their behalf. One of his first acts was to give Mary Musgrove Bosomworth Ossabaw, St. Catherine's and Sapelo Islands. The proclamation dated December 14, 1747, was addressed to "the subjects of the Crown of Great Britain." The document was also signed by leaders of various Creek towns.

Why did Malatchi do this? Certainly, Mary's coaxing had a lot to do with it. Mary had a prominent place in the Creek capitol city of Coweta, where she was born. But Malatchi was following Tomochichi, who also thought it was important to place these islands in Mary's care. The islands were some of the favorite preserves of the Creeks. It is likely that the chiefs thought Mary could preserve these islands from the greedy hands of the British. And since the British valued private property, giving the islands as private land to Mary was a move that the British would respect.

Malatchi was also pronouncing his foreign policy as one that would work to fight for the rights of Indians to use their lands as they felt. This instigated one of the biggest incidents between the Creeks and Savannah's leadership. In the summer of 1749, Malatchi traveled with Creek warriors and leaders—as well as Mary and her husband, Thomas Bosomworth—to Savannah. Malatchi had advocated on behalf of Senauki (the wife of Tomochichi), but the British denied her rights. He was now traveling to argue Mary's case and receive gifts from the British. The Europeans used gifts as a way to gain the loyalties of the Indians. The Indians desired and were even a little dependent on these presents.

As was the custom for the Indians, he stayed at Cowpens (Mary's trading post) and waited for the colonists to invite him into the city. They waited several days before offering the invitation, which deeply offended Malatchi. Things would not get much better. Mary and the colonists were at odds, and she was even placed in jail. Malatchi worried about the Creeks he had brought with him; Mary was caught in quite the bind. Malatchi, who was a constant supporter of Mary's, betrayed her for a moment in the squabbling between the colonists, Coweta Creeks and Mary.

The acting governor, William Stephens, goaded Malatchi by asking him if he or Mary was the chief. In what was certainly not one of his finest moments, Malatchi called Mary an "old woman." He also denounced any importance she had and declared he was chief. One can imagine the psychology at play here. Malatchi, who had to wait for his brother, his brother's mentor and then Chigelley to die before he could be the chief, was probably sensitive about his title. He had already been slighted by the colonists while he awaited their invitation to enter the town. Now, in front of the other micos and his warriors, his chiefdom was being challenged or at least suggested it was weak. He felt a need to assert his place. He accepted the gifts Mary and her husband had arranged to have to share with the Creeks (the colonists were refusing to give Mary any of the gifts). In the verbal exchanges Malatchi had with Governor Stephens, he convinced him to finally declare the islands Creek land. He left Savannah angrily but felt he had done the best for his Creek brethren in what was a bad situation. He and Mary reconciled, and he never betrayed her again. In the future, he showed constant support for her in her endeavor to gain the lands she had been promised.

After this unseemly meeting with the Savannah leadership, Malatchi began to deal more with the French. But in keeping with his father's diplomacy he changed his focus from Savannah as his primary British contact and instead strengthened his ties with the British in Charleston. The time of the Tomochichi and Oglethorpe union was past, and the new leadership was proving to be a threat to the Creek land. One of the ongoing diplomatic challenges for the Creeks was that Charleston and Savannah had different approaches toward the Creeks according to each new governor the cities had. This meant that the policies of the two cities changed accordingly. At this point, there was no unified voice of the British. Malatchi, angry and not confident in the Savannah leadership, needed to create stronger ties with the other local colony, Charleston, with which he hoped to work more amicably. Of course, the Creeks had to continue to maintain diplomatic channels of communication with Savannah, but for the season, Malatchi played the cities against each other.

Malatchi continued to rule until his death in 1756. He led the Creeks for ten years. His leadership was remembered with veneration, as he had maintained the Brim dynasty and policy of neutrality. Malatchi's son was viewed as a weak leader, and Coweta was no longer the capitol. And with him ended the Brim dynasty. But Malatchi had completed his long-held dream of being as good a mico as his father had been.

9

SENAUKI, THE GOOD MOTHER

Senauki was a prominent player among the Yamacraws. Yet because she was a woman, her activities were not always written down. She was the wife of Tomochichi. She was also the one through which, in Creek life, the hereditary line was recorded. As the wife of the mico, she was one of the leaders who kept the tribe together. She managed the agricultural life of the family and the town's reserve of food. She was the primary link between her family and the British traders. As the wife of the mico, she—much like our First Ladies—had the power of the mico's ear in the privacy of their home. So, in the life of the Yamacraws, she was, if not a vocal leader, certainly a silent leader. As with Mary Musgrove, women were allowed to participate in tribal debates, although this was rare. The Creeks divided spheres of influence between the man and woman, but they viewed these spheres as economic functions and not cultural mores. It is only after several years of contact with the British that women's roles become more subservient. Hunting, especially for deerskins for the British and not for the use of the family and tribe, enacted a change in the household economy and thus the role of women in the family and community. Men's work became the primary source of acquiring trade goods, as the Creeks slowly became more economically dependent on the Europeans. The men began to interact with traders more, and their ability to hunt became the more important function for the familial and tribal economy.

Tomochichi's heir came from Senauki's side of the family. The heirs always came from the maternal line. Usually, this would have been the child

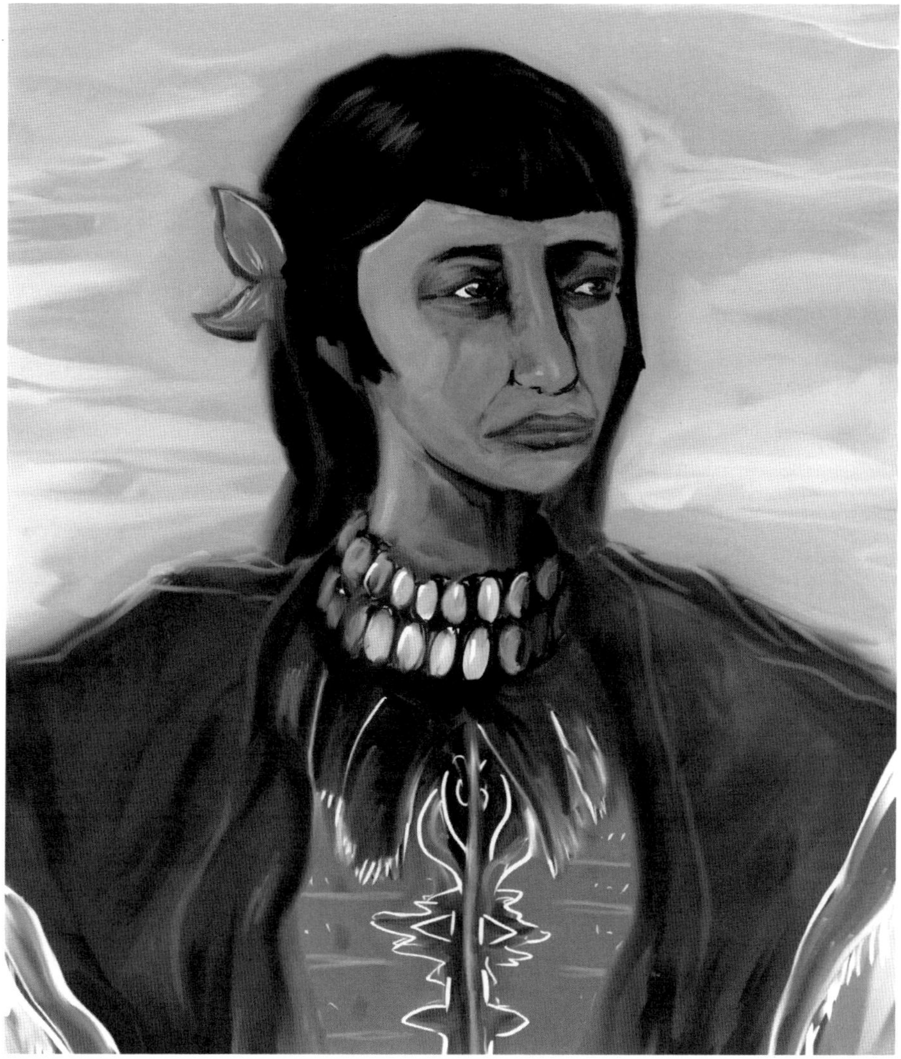

Painting of Senauki. *Art of Philip Freeman.*

of Tomochichi and Senauki, but since they had no children, Toonahowi was chosen. He was often referred to as a nephew but appears to be Senauki's grandson through her daughter. Why Tomochichi and Senauki did not have children of their own is not known.

But Senauki, in the early days of the colony, was the hostess for the colonists in this new and strange land. Women in the Creek culture were to welcome strangers. That is why she was the one bearing gifts of milk and honey when John Wesley first came to the colony. When micos from other tribes came to meet and discuss with Tomochichi and Oglethorpe, she was behind the scenes making sure that housing, food, drink and other details were handled in an appropriate manner.

Tomochichi included her in many events, because in Creek culture, the presence of a woman represented the peaceful nature of the meeting. One could reasonably assume that when Tomochichi was an outcast, Senauki was a source of comfort and guidance. And when they formed a new tribe that was not Creek, the two of them would have leaned on each other for counsel. Maybe more importantly, Senauki was essential to maintaining ties with the Creeks. She had family still in the Creek Nation, and as one of the matrilineal heads of a clan, she was important to Tomochichi as he tried to restore his and the Yamacraws' ties with the Creeks.

For all these reasons, Senauki was present for most of the major events of Tomochichi's encounters with the colonists. She was there when they first met the colonists and Oglethorpe. She attended church services he attended. She was there at the first meeting with John Wesley. She traveled to England. She was at Tomochichi's bedside when he died and attended the English funeral for Tomochichi when he was buried in Wright Square.

On the visit to England, the trustees used Senauki and Tomochichi's marriage as signs of the civilized nature of the Creeks in an attempt to allay the fears that the English had about the wild country of America. Most importantly, in the famous painting by William Verelst of the Creek micos and the trustees meeting, she is the only woman depicted. In the image, Senauki is wearing a petticoat and a bow in her hair. This choice of British fashion emphasized their willingness and ability to accept British culture. Notably, Tomochichi—as leader of the Creek delegation—is shown wearing his native clothing. Thus a balance is struck between the willingness to learn from the British but the pride and equal footing the Creeks saw themselves as having. Senauki was one of only two Indian women to travel to England during the colonial period. The other was Pocahontas.

The important nature of Senauki's role became evident when they returned to Georgia. A meeting with Creek leaders, welcoming Tomochichi back in the Creek fold as the main liaison between the Creeks and British, was held. During this meeting, Chigelley, the headman of Coweta (until Malatchi was of age), declared her "the mother of all Creeks." This designation, although probably hyperbole, recognized her as the lineage of the Creeks' future. She may have played a minor role in

British thinking, but in the Creek world, women in general and Senauki in particular played major roles.

One of the unspoken roles she had when the men were gone hunting, scouting, determining where to build forts and roads or even what was the boundary of Georgia, was the core leader at home. This more than likely meant she was the voice in grievances and the leader in joint ventures between the Creeks and colonists on Tomochichi's frequent trips away. She was not only the Creek mother at this time but also the mother of the early colonists.

After Tomochichi died and Oglethorpe returned to England, Senauki continued to live on traditional Yamacraw lands. But trouble soon came her way, as the new colonists were less friendly to the Creeks as they became more independent. She could have returned to a Creek village but stayed, probably to assist Toonahowi in his transition from heir to mico. It was her home and the place of Tomochichi's grave. She also was a good friend to Mary Musgrove. But the new generation of colonists did not respect the boundaries of the Yamacraw lands. The colonists were continually expanding west, regardless of what treaties and whatever enforcement the British government made.

Soon, they were pilfering timber and, on occasion, livestock from Senauki's lands. She likely seemed an easy target, an old Indian women living by herself. In December 1746, she filed a complaint with the magistrates of the Georgia colony. She stated that in the treaty of 1733, she was granted this land. This was four years after the death of Toonahowi. The Yamacraws were dispersing among other tribes after the early death of Toonahowi and the onslaught of settlers on their land. Malatchi, now the mico of Coweta, spoke on her behalf, as did the mico Santachee, who had traveled to England with her so many years ago. But the words of an Indian were no longer admitted in court, as they had been in the past. William Stephens, the president of Georgia, refused to consider this claim from an old Indian woman. They needed a Christian to speak on her behalf. Trying to redeem a bad situation, Malatchi and Senauki asked for presents for her injuries if nothing else. They were denied.

This incident was probably the final impetus for the Yamacraws departure and dispersal among other tribes. If the British treated Senauki this way, what chance did they have? Senauki's claims were at first submitted when the Creeks defended Mary and her claims, but later, they appeared to have been dropped. Stephens was a thorn in the flesh of Mary Musgrove in her later claims for her lands. The forward march of the colonists through the Creek land had started and would not stop until the Creeks were removed to Oklahoma (even there, they had to forfeit land promised them, as new settlers in Oklahoma wanted it, too).

It is not known when Senauki died, but there are no records of her in the 1750s. Thus, we might assume her death was in the late 1740s. Senauki's burial place is not known. If she was buried close to her home, her grave would not have been marked to prevent it from desecration. Today, she is the least studied and known of the Savannah Native American leaders who first encountered the colonists.

10

MARY MUSGROVE, THE WOMAN WHO RAN WITH THE WOLVES

Mary Musgrove lived in two worlds, and by the end of her life, despite all odds, she mastered them both. As Atlas did, she stood across expanses to hold up her world. She was in business in a time when women were to be in the domestic sphere. She lived as both British citizen and Creek woman. She traversed the disputed land where the French, Spanish and British laid claim. She married and loved three men of different backgrounds and class. She was a natural-born linguist, mastering both Muskogee and English. Her whole life, she challenged the norms of her day. In the end, after much struggle, she became one of the wealthiest women Georgia and America had ever known.

Mary was born in the Creek village of Coweta to a Creek mother and an English father. The year was about 1700. Coweta was the "lead" town for the Lower Creeks. Her mother was from the clan family of the great Brim, a mico held in high esteem by both the Creek and English. Brim helped strengthen the loose confederacy known as the Creeks to give a political response to the growing infiltration of the British colonies into Native American land. When the Creeks were set back on their heels after their loss of the Yamasee War, he led with a calm, steady hand through the murky waters in which they found themselves. His son Malatchi was groomed to replace him, and Brim's brother Chigelley stood in for Malatchi until he came of age. Malatchi played an important part in Mary's life. It is thought by some that Malatchi was Mary's younger cousin.

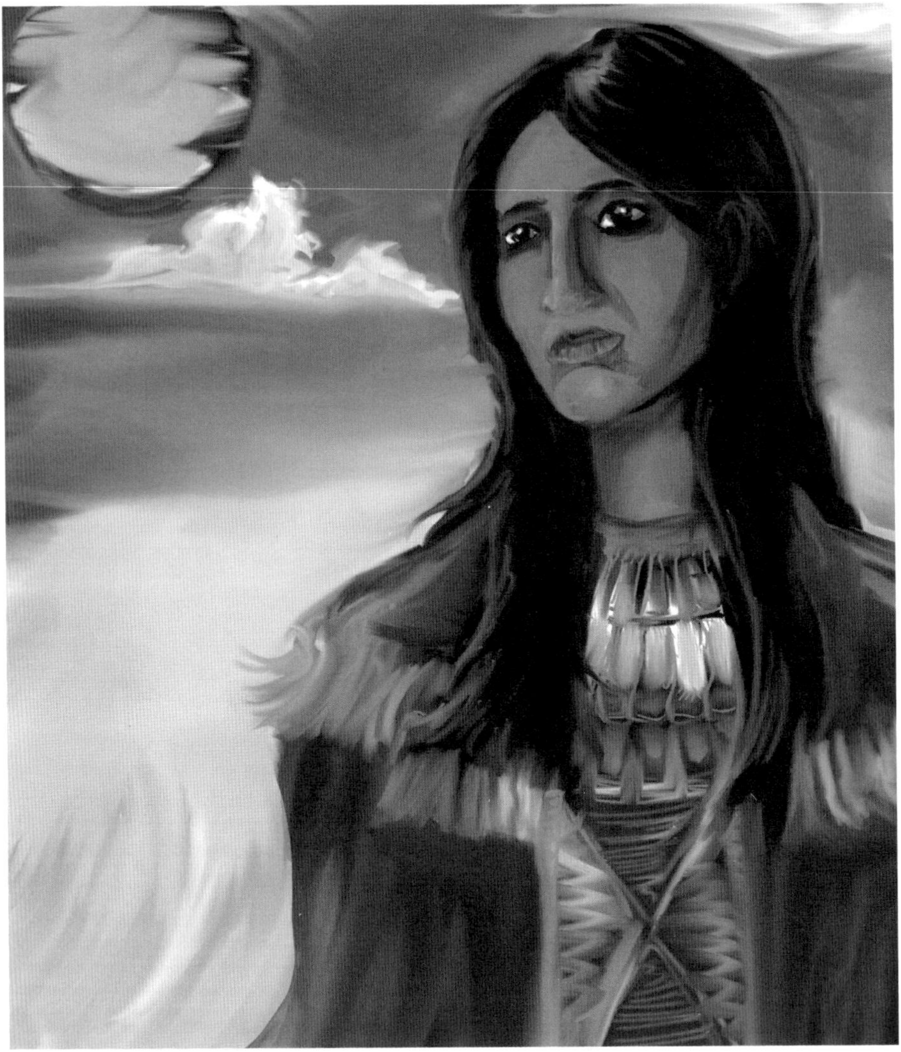

Painting of Mary Musgrove. *Art of Philip Freeman.*

Her father, Edward Griffith, was a deerskin trader. He was one of the few traders the Creeks felt dealt with them fairly. He probably married out of love and political necessity. The Creeks and traders alike not only accepted these marriages but also saw them as tightening the bonds between the British and Creeks. In the frontier, the traders were vastly outnumbered and needed a talwa, or clan, to act as protectorates to survive. The traders were conduits between the British cities of Charleston and Savannah and the Creeks. More and more, the Creeks found their economy reliant on the trade with British colonists for British goods.

When Mary was seven, her mother died. Her father took her from the Creeks to a frontier town called Pon Pon. Pon Pon was one of the new Anglican parishes the South Carolinians established on the frontier edge. This change of scenery propelled young Mary into a totally different world. The language, buildings, clothes and customs were different. Here, Anglican Christianity was the practice. She was baptized during her stay in Pon Pon and received an English education. Women did not have the same roles as they did in Creek society. Creek society was matrilineal, and while the men and women had different spheres, the women were treated as partners. In England, women were limited to the domestic sphere, which was considered a lesser world. However, the lines blurred out of necessity the further you were removed from the cities and in the wilderness.

Mary also met other *mestizos* who would become her lifelong friends. Mestizos was the name given to people of racially mixed parentage. She found fellow mestizos with whom to play, study and live. She would have, during this time, met the colonists' children who had no experience with the foreign culture of the Native Americans. But more importantly, Pon Pon was not far from the Creeks. This enabled her to maintain a

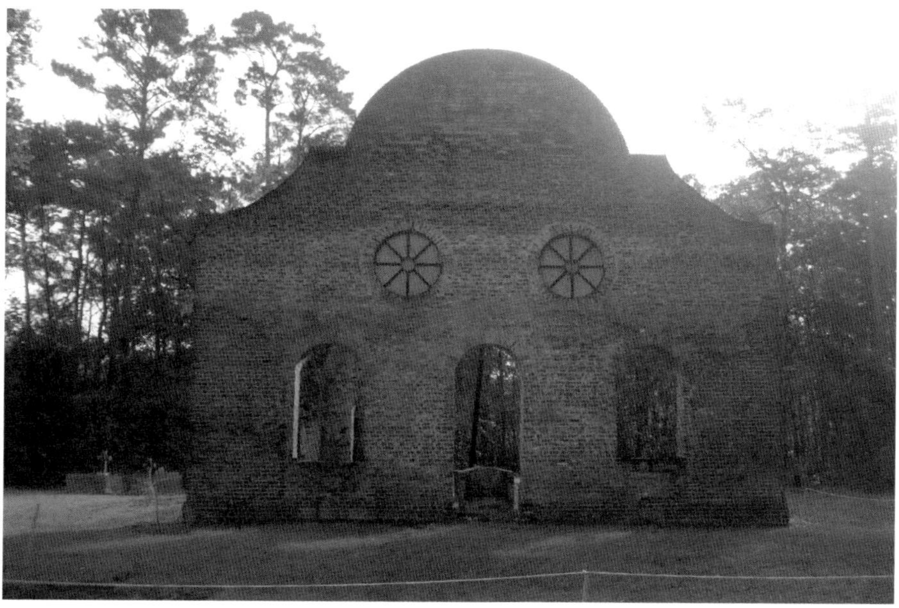

Chapel of ease at Pon Pon where Mary and John lived. *Author's collection.*

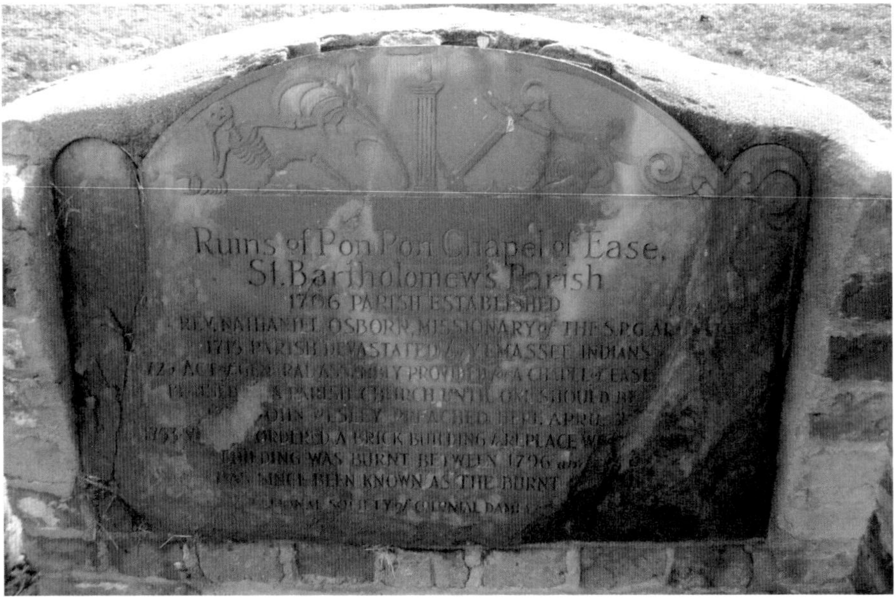

Plaque at chapel of ease at Pon Pon. *Author's collection.*

connection with her Creek heritage. In fact, the small village of Pon Pon could be seen as a shining example of the diversity of the newly forming colony. Here French, British, blacks, Indians and mestizos met and lived together. This was good preparation for the diplomatic work Mary would one day do.

It was here in Pon Pon that Mary lived when the Yamasee War started. Despite her Creek heritage, she fled with the other colonists to Charleston. As in most wars, there was no time for distinctions between friend and foe. It is believed that her father was killed in the early days, as the Creeks and Yamasees took control of the villages on the frontier. Mary was left an orphan. She lived with her aunt for the next several years.

It was during a sojourn back to Pon Pon that she met her first husband, John Musgrove. He was a mestizo too. John's father was a captain of the South Carolina Militia with some land and therefore was of some prominence. His mother was an Indian. Although he was raised in a European world, he was not as literate as Mary. Yet when the British went to battle, he fought with the Creeks alongside the British. The two fell in love and began to create a home for themselves. Many have claimed Mary married to promote herself in British society, but it is more likely she felt an affinity for this man with a similar background and seemingly

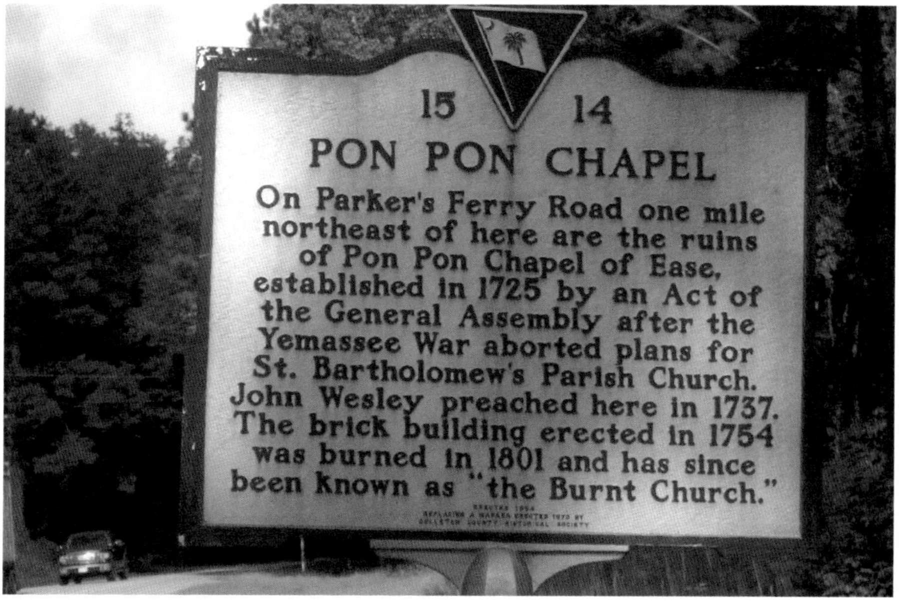

Marker near Walterboro, South Carolina, about Pon Pon Chapel. *Author's collection.*

similar dreams. So it would not have been a far stretch to assume she would feel most comfortable at this stage of her life with someone whose life experience was the same.

John and Mary's homesteading was successful. They moved to St. Bartholomew Parish with other mestizos. They farmed more than traded at this point of their lives. They grew rice, corn and other common crops. They were a bit unusual in that they raised cattle, a trade John had picked up from his father. They also had two slaves. Nothing in their Creek or European backgrounds felt ill at ease with slavery. To the Musgroves, the moral question was more focused on how you treated your slaves. Through the years, they grew their landholdings to well over five hundred acres. John also supplemented his income by working with the South Carolina Militia, leaving Mary at home in charge of their holdings for long periods of time. She was slowly gaining skills that would later prove beneficial.

In June 1732, Upper and Lower Creeks went to Charleston for a peace treaty. Tomochichi was present at the same meeting, asking for permission (or agreement, according to your perspective) to settle in the disputed lands. As part of this treaty, it was agreed that Tomochichi and his new tribe, the Yamacraws, along with the Musgroves, would move to Yamacraw Bluff. The South Carolinians wanted to create more trade with the Creeks and lay claim to land that was at least for the Europeans a no-man's land. The Musgroves were to be the arbitrator between British and Creek trade. Tomochichi, for his part, had the essential right of first refusal for all British goods and was close at hand to be first in line with his goods to sell to the colonists.

The two had barely settled on Yamacraw Bluff when the ship *Anne* landed on January 11, 1733, in Charleston. James Oglethorpe had come to set up the colony of Georgia. Oglethorpe set sail with up-and-coming William Bull of Charleston, who later served as governor of South Carolina. Bull, who was familiar with the territory, was to show Oglethorpe different places on the coast where he might build his first settlement. He also acted as engineer for what is now called the Oglethorpe Plan for the new city, Savannah. Oglethorpe, upon seeing Yamacraw Bluff, decided this would be ideal for his new settlement. The only problem was Tomochichi and the Yamacraws, as well as Mary and John, were already settled there. One can assume that at first, both of these groups were not pleased with Oglethorpe's choice.

Tomochichi had to be especially alarmed that his first experience with the new Georgia colonists was displacement. He was surely aware of the ongoing issues with the colonists' insatiable need for more and more land. As for Mary and John, they had left their property in South Carolina (although they had kept some land from their original holdings there) to settle anew, and within two years, they were being uprooted. But they each apparently also saw possibilities. It was probably here that Mary's legendary diplomatic skills were first on display, as she surely was an asset in helping to persuade Tomochichi and the Yamacraws to relinquish the land to the colonists. Thus began the role of John and Mary as the chosen interpreters for Oglethorpe.

Tomochichi moved to what was later referred to as the Irene Mounds, and not far away (about one mile), Mary and John set up their new trading post, called Cowpens. It is from Cowpens that Mary's influence grew. Cowpens became the everyday meeting place for the colonists and the Indians. One of the reasons for this was, although alcohol was not allowed in the colony, Cowpens was not under this restriction and sold rum. So Cowpens was a trading post and part bar, much to the chagrin of Oglethorpe, to be sure.

During the first few years of the settling of Savannah, John was the primary interpreter for Oglethorpe. Mary was the keeper of the home, albeit Cowpens was not your typical home. John, though not as fluent as Mary, was utilized because of a male bias but also because he could be and was used as a soldier. But Mary acted more as an influence on Tomochichi and the Yamacraws to learn and adjust to British culture. She was the one who regularly brought Yamacraws to attend worship services in Savannah. The church attendance of the Yamacraws caused quite a stir in Savannah, as many colonists received their first up-close view of an Indian. But the greatest stir was when Tomochichi, the mico, attended the service. The conversion rate among the Yamacraws seems to be close to, if not totally, nil. Tomochichi's attendance could be seen as an observation of the culture of these people who were now his neighbors, more than any great need for another belief system. Mary became heir Toonahowi's tutor as well.

Mary and John's wealth continued to grow. They now had three Indian slaves. While it was illegal to have African slaves in the new colony, the use of Indian slaves was not outlawed. John traveled to England with Oglethorpe and Tomochichi in 1734. While there, John continued his new struggle with alcohol and became, on at least one occasion, unable to perform his duties. But most importantly for Mary's story, while there, he purchased an indentured servant named Jacob Matthews, who returned with him to Cowpens.

It was during John's visit to England that Mary faced her first challenge to her place in the world. John left Joseph Watson in charge of their trade while he was away. Watson almost immediately began to make off-the-book side deals for himself with other traders. Mary, who was being used more as an interpreter while John was away, was also gaining more prominence. She challenged Watson about his business dealings. For her efforts, he began a campaign of slander against her, denouncing his employer as a witch, sexually promiscuous and unfaithful to John. These charges, while never proved, were to follow Mary for the rest of her life. Watson was cheating the Musgroves and became a raging alcoholic as well. Watson began to make unwelcome advances toward Indian women who came to Cowpens to trade, even some who were married. The Indians, infuriated by his behavior, made an attempt to kill Watson, but Mary intervened and saved his life. Mary may have saved his life, but she also took him to court and Watson was jailed for all his misbehaviors. Mary was left in charge of the trade of Cowpens. For a woman and mestizo to win a case against an English man was quite unusual, but Mary meticulously documented all Cowpens business. Her prowess as a businesswoman became evident. Also, it should be noted here that Mary was quite articulate, as it is her voice that time and time again pacified the Indians and challenged the English to do right by her and her mother's people. At one point, Watson was released from jail and, angry at Mary, drew a gun on her. The tenacious Mary disarmed and subdued him. Watson slandered her even worse after this event. He used the fact of Mary and John's mixed heritage against them. He remained Mary's foe for the rest of her life.

One can imagine that Mary was glad to see John return from England. Although he would have heard the rumors about Mary, it appears he found no credence to them, as their happy marriage continued. But their union most certainly changed; Mary was a businesswoman now. She was never a wallflower but, more than likely, felt freer to assert herself in the nondomestic spheres of their life together. It is certain that Mary took a bigger part in the business, because her record keeping continued, and it proved valuable in her later claims for property and land from England. Also, as a payment for his services in England, John received five hundred acres of land.

In the year 1735, tragedy struck. John and her two sons died, leaving Mary in charge of Cowpens. The problem was that in English law, a woman could not inherit property. It was to return to the Crown. This law played a prominent role later in Mary's ongoing battle with Georgia and England for her property and wages.

But John Musgrove's death broke her heart. John Wesley, who was the clergy in charge of the religious affairs of Georgia and later the founder of the Methodist denomination, had befriended Mary. After paying her a bereavement visit at Cowpens, he was very much worried about her emotional and spiritual health. Wesley, who had several previous personal conversations about their respective faiths, knew Mary well. Mary, who was apparently a woman of action, was inert and incapable of doing her regular business. Wesley wrote in his diary that he must make a return visit to her soon. Obviously, Mary had loved John and was a caring mother, although she would later be accused of only being concerned about money and never having loved any of her husbands.

Her relationship with Wesley should serve as notice that Mary had a prominent stature in Georgia. When Wesley first arrived in Savannah, Tomochichi, Senauki and Mary met him with milk and honey to represent the Promised Land in which he had arrived. Certainly, the idea of this gift was made by the Anglican Mary. But it was also Mary to whom Wesley entrusted one of his priests to learn Muskogee. Two Moravians also joined the "classes." The hope was that they would be able to translate the Bible into the Muskogee language. Out of this venture would come the "Musgrove vocabulary." This is the only surviving attempt to translate Muskogee, a verbal, not written, language, into English and German. (The Moravians spoke German.)

Mary married the servant her deceased husband brought back from England, Jacob Matthews. Many accused Jacob of using Mary to lift his status in life. But it is just as likely Mary married him to ensure her claim to the land and property that John and she had accumulated. It is probable that Matthews and Mary became close during her mourning time. At Cowpens, even though there were distinctions, everyone was treated as family. If Mary was as immobilized as Wesley noted, she would have needed someone to lean on for help with running the trading post and farm. It should be noted that Wesley refused to marry the two. He did not think Matthews sufficiently Anglican enough to marry them. (It should be said here that Mary's Anglican faith was not challenged.) Since Wesley was the religious authority of Georgia, this was a huge impediment to their union. So Mary recruited the Salzburger minister John Boltzius to go to Savannah with her and convince Wesley to wed her and Matthews. Along the way, they stopped in Purrysburg, South Carolina. We do not know for sure, but Mary likely knew, through friends, that the French preacher Henry Chiffele there had married other couples Wesley had refused to marry. Instead of continuing to Savannah, she was wedded to Matthews by Chiffele. All of this effort to marry Matthews indicates that Mary, who could have probably had other men, was fond of this particular man.

This did not sit well with Wesley. When it came time for one of Mary's worker's babies to be baptized, Wesley refused to allow Matthews to stand as a godparent for the baby during the ceremony. This led Mary to join in a formal complaint with others against Wesley for his overly pious actions. These complaints led to Wesley leaving Savannah.

Mary did one other thing to ensure her claim to her property. She had a feast with Tomochichi and William Stephens, the new secretary of the colony, and others in attendance. Tomochichi, wanting to thank Mary for her service to the Yamacraws, granted her the land on which they feasted, which once was inhabited by the Yamacraws. Stephens, who had not known the purpose of the meeting, sat by as Tomochichi made this grant of land to Mary. Tomochichi, fully aware of the magnitude of his actions, stated that he hoped the trustees would not be upset. He went on to state he expected that grazing cattle and other uses by the colonists on Creek land would stop. Stephens, the new kid in town, gave a reluctant and unsure yes to this request. This grant of land led Mary to become persona non grata with the Georgia officials, as she time and time again had to lay claim for either payment for the land or the return of the land to her. Even Oglethorpe, who had acknowledged Mary's invaluable service to the colony, did not assist her in securing this land request because he was not sure of the legalities of Tomochichi's gift in the first place.

In 1738, Oglethorpe needed Mary's guidance and influence, as he asserted the English claim to the disputed lands of Georgia over the Spanish in Florida. To help in this cause, she started another trade center called Mount Venture on the Altahama River, closer to Fort Frederica on St. Simons Island. Here, Oglethorpe had easier access to Mary as a translator and a strategic source of information-gathering from the Indians and traders who came to Mount Venture. Mary was also given a lot with a house in Fort Frederica to use when her services were needed for an extended amount of time. The battle with Spain for territory was about to commence.

During this time, Oglethorpe signed a treaty in Coweta, Mary's birthplace, on August 21, 1739, establishing clear lines where the British were allowed to settle. Tomochichi was not present at this meeting due to an illness that would eventually lead to his death. This treaty would, without Mary's permission, grant the colonists her land that was given to her by Tomochichi. Was Oglethorpe acting duplicitously by this action? Probably not. The treaty was in large part a reiteration of the 1733 treaty. Oglethorpe, while aware of Tomochichi's gift of land to Mary, was not there when the grant was made. Also, Tomochichi was not there to clarify or challenge the treaty and neither was Toonahowi, his groomed successor, who had stayed to be at Tomochichi's deathbed. But Tomochichi was there for the signing of the 1733 treaty. Most of the land added to the new treaty was the coastal land south of Savannah, which the colonists were already occupying. Add to this the fact that Creek view of ownership of land was so different from the British, the Creeks probably saw no problem with granting this land to the colonists. After all, land was for communal use first and personal use second. But this treaty was a thorn in Mary's side as she tried to claim her land.

Oglethorpe was ready to invade Florida and needed volunteers to help him. Mary was influential in recruiting for Oglethorpe's military surge into Florida to take St. Augustine. She recruited people from her Pon Pon days living in South Carolina, her brother Edward Griffith, as well as Creeks she knew. Oglethorpe's impetus for starting the invasion was that the European War of Jenkin's Ear between Spain and England had begun. The plan was for the British navy to blockade St. Augustine and for him to lay siege. The blockade did not work, and Oglethorpe had to withdraw, but while retreating, his troops captured Fort Mose from the Spanish. It lay two miles north of St. Augustine. He left a contingent of his troops there to hold the fort. This was a critical mistake on his part. The Spanish mustered 300 men and attacked the 170 men inside. The British troops were caught unawares and totally annihilated. Mary lost her brother, Pon Pon friends and Creek relatives in the disaster. She was devastated. Oglethorpe was roundly criticized for his strategic mistake. Mary held a silent grudge against Oglethorpe for this critical error. Once again, Mary suffered a great loss. She left for Coweta to regain her bearings. It seems Mary felt more at home with her Indian kin in times of sorrow and grief.

Of all the things Jacob Matthews offered Mary, probably the most significant was his introduction of her to a group called the "Malcontents." The economy was not doing well, and Oglethorpe's military setbacks had made many in the colony disgruntled. They made appeals to the courts and wrote pamphlets for change. The Malcontents were Georgia colonists who were opposed to the rules and structures of the colony and wanted reform. They became most visible at this time in the colony's history. Some of the changes they espoused were rescinding the prohibition to slavery, landholding limitations, the ending of the laws that did not permit women to inherit land and an elected assembly for Georgia, as every other colony had.

While Mary never directly joined the group, Matthews was an active participant. Their headquarters of sorts was Cowpens. This allowed them to plan and organize out of sight of the royal government. It is unlikely that, if Mary did not tacitly support the group, she would have allowed them to meet at Cowpens and taken on the hostess role for them while they stayed there. Certainly, many of their goals ran congruent with Mary's personal interests.

Mary, at this time, also began to challenge the religious and social norms of the Fort Frederica colonists. Mary, who was constantly bringing her newborn Creek kin to be baptized into the church, chose a frowned-upon Malcontent minister to perform the baptisms. Mary challenged the colonists mores when two women were cast out of Savannah because they were pregnant and single. Mary took them in, and they lived at Mount Venture. This would have been a challenge to the governmental authorities, who probably would have taken the children from them and exiled the women. She also became a stronger advocate for Indians against their British neighbors. Arguing cases regarding horses that had been promised but never delivered, Mary was learning from the Malcontents how to subtly and not so subtly challenge the authorities through actions, organizing and the courts. All these skills she utilized to keep her land and money claims before the royal government.

In October 1741, Mary and Jacob asked for 450 of the thousands of acres granted to her by Tomochichi and recompense for the work she had done for the government. This infuriated the Savannah government and elite, who were already prone to dislike the Malcontent and whore-harborer. Tomochichi's land gift, they said, was illegal, because only the colonial government could give land away. Her claim challenged the British governmental structure, arguing that Indian governance could grant land too. She brought with her an agreement of Creek leaders that had been made with Oglethorpe in attendance, granting this land. They also told Mary that she had, as far as they were concerned, been paid for her services. But because Oglethorpe had been present at the grant, they allowed him to make final judgment—but Oglethorpe was in England. Although it did not look good, the final decision was left pending.

Jacob Matthews had been jailed several times for various Malcontents' issues. It was during the trial for Mary's property and his trial for being a "public nuisance" that he was jailed once again. His trial had potential for a lengthy jail time, but he was eventually released. Yet because of the stress, the unsanitary jail or something else, he was very sick. He died several days after being released. Mary was once again a widow. Between the Fort Mose incident, the disagreement over her land grant and now the treatment and death of Jacob, one could expect Mary to stop assisting the colonists. Yet she continued to assist the colonies whenever she could.

Mary was in possession of two trading posts and a farm of nearly five hundred acres at Cowpens that she and John Musgrove had next to the trading post. She had yet to receive any compensation for the land Tomochichi presented her or her past services. Because of her travels back and forth to Fort Frederica to assist Oglethorpe, her finances were hurting. The farm fields had not been planted in several years. She slowly began to rebuild her fortune. She stayed in Cowpens hoping to plant in the fields. Yet merely two weeks after Jacob died, Oglethorpe asked Mary to come to Fort Frederica. The War of Jenkin's Ear was still on, and it had become clear that the long-awaited Spanish invasion was imminent. This was one of the few times Mary denied Oglethorpe's request. Her grief and need to look after her finances were too pressing.

The Spanish, with fifty ships and two thousand troops, did indeed invade St. Simons on July 5, but by July 7, Oglethorpe and his troops had thwarted the attack and the Spanish retreated, never to return. It was a huge military victory for Oglethorpe, rescuing his reputation after the Fort Mose slaughter of his men. Toonahowi was there and distinguished himself in battle.

Oglethorpe wrote Mary to tell her of his victory. He told her in the Creek sense of reckoning vengeance against the Spaniards for her lost kin at Fort Mose had been made fulfilled. Mary, while she still did not travel to Fort Frederica, continued to recruit Creek braves to assist Oglethorpe.

It was good that Mary had not joined Oglethorpe. In November, a Spanish and Yamasee party attacked Mount Venture, destroying the site and killing one of the mothers and her child, whom Mary rescued from social ostracism. This attack put a huge dent in Mary's fortune and added to her grief.

The destruction of Mount Venture resulted in Mary finally traveling to Fort Frederica to answer Oglethorpe's call for help. The Spanish attack caused Creek braves, anxious to have revenge for Mary's sake, to come in droves to fight with Oglethorpe. It also opened the door to a chance meeting with Thomas Bosomworth, her next husband.

Bosomworth was an Anglican priest from Yorkshire, England, who had risen to a prominent stature in the community. He had a university education and was versed in Latin. This made him one of the leading young gentlemen of the colony. He was also twenty years younger than Mary. His youthfulness and his pronounced desire to make something of himself made many people think of him as a sort who married Mary for her fortune and influence. But it is Mary's fortune and influence that would beg to differ with this. She could have had any number of men. Mary was, one can assume, in need of someone prominent to match her own status. They also had the similarity of rags-to-riches backgrounds and a certain comfort with rabble-rousing. Whatever the reason, they were quickly married after their first meeting on July 9, 1744. This marriage placed Mary in the highest echelons of colonial society. A landed woman married to an educated priest. The Savannah community was scandalized.

In 1743, Joseph Watson, Mary's old nemesis, petitioned for one hundred acres of Mary's land while he was in England. Watson claimed Mary was cheating the Indians and the British in her trade deals. He also said that unlike the good English man he was, she was a heathen. Watson was trying to play on the prejudices of the British. But upon his return, he was denied Mary Bosomworth's land and a trader's license to compete with her business interests. When he was denied the license, he began an illegal trade business and began to slander Mary, as was his habit. Mary and Thomas took Watson to court, where he lost the case. He paid a fine and was released from jail.

This incident led Mary to decide once again to make an appeal for her land and the pay she felt she had coming to her. This would start a ten-year battle, as Mary took on the Savannahians, trustees, parliament and even the king of England. The "uppitiness" of a Creek woman challenging all these institutions was not favorably viewed by the citizens of Savannah. Needless to say, she and Thomas became pariahs in the Savannah community during this time.

Thomas approached William Stephens, the president of the Georgia province, with new claims for Mary. She was now broadening her compensation for crops, beef provided to the colonists before they had their own cattle and other items she had given the struggling colonists. Stephens, who did not necessarily know of these issues, brushed Thomas aside, saying he would look into the matter. Meanwhile, Thomas had accrued significant debt. Mary's finances after Mount Venture were not as stable as they once were. She needed the land and money she was due. It was no longer only justice she sought.

Fortuitously, at this time, Oglethorpe wrote the couple a letter stating that he would love to see them in London and if they needed help to let him know. Thomas decided to go to London to seek Oglethorpe's assistance. In order not to be prevented from traveling abroad by his lenders, he snuck off to Charleston, took a ship and arrived in London in July 1745. Mary stayed home to run Cowpens. Mary had provided Thomas with records of her old and new claims that had not been paid. Oglethorpe said he would help. Meanwhile, he allowed the couple to have up to a thousand pounds of credit on his account. He also wrote William Horton, his replacement at Fort Frederica, that if he could, he should look into paying Mary for past services. But when the case went before the trustees, unfortunately, Oglethorpe was facing court-martial for dereliction of duty by an officer in his Georgian army. This made him unable to speak on her account. But an old enemy, Thomas Jones, spoke against her, and the trustees referred the case back to the president of Georgia. Mary and Thomas were back to square one.

Mary and Thomas, knowing they were not favored in Savannah, began strategic moves to build allies. Mary, who had learned politics by watching the Malcontents, and Thomas, with his legal mind, challenged the British laws that were in Mary's way to settle her land dispute. They were determined the British would yield. Acting as though the land dispute was a fait accompli in their favor, they built a home on Cumberland Island. The coastal islands had long been the Creeks' hunting and fishing preserves. This brought them closer (than Savannah or Cowpens) to Fort Frederica, where they had allies. At Federica, William Horton (Oglethorpe's military replacement) knew of the invaluable services Mary provided. They also opened another trading post on the Altamaha River, which brought Mary in closer contact with her Creek friends. Malatchi was a regular visitor at the Altamaha trading post. As the mico of Coweta and Mary's kin, he agreed to help Mary with her pleas to the British. He did this, one would suppose, because of kindred ties but also because Mary's case had relevance to other Creek issues of land. Malatchi was interested in the Creeks' grievances being addressed too.

The Creeks were now battling for their land, as the colonists were moving westward to settle. They complained to the magistrate, who said unless they had Christian testimony to substantiate their claims, he would not hear them. They did not, and the court ignored them. This angered the Creeks, who previously did not need Christian testimony. This was a sign that the Creeks were being treated as an underclass.

Malatchi now challenged the white man and his towns. The winds of war were in the air. Malatchi, because of his strong speeches, was no longer a welcomed figure in the cities. Mary gave a speech at the Altamaha trading post with Malatchi present, declaring that the British were using paper to take away Creek lands and that Oglethorpe had not always been a faithful friend of the Indians. Mary was now identifying strongly with the Indians as her people.

After the Georgia provincial court had rebuked her claims a few more times, she decided to use her ally, William Horton, to go over the provincial governments and the trustees' heads. She asked Horton to deliver a letter and his support to the Secretary of State to King George II. This was in 1747, a year that Malatchi was openly courting a relationship with the French, a move that further alarmed the colonists. Mary used this in her testimony, saying she was the only one who might prevent an alliance from happening. For all their renewed efforts, Mary and Thomas were rewarded by being called traitors.

Thomas called on his brother Abraham to go to Coweta and attain an affidavit from traders espousing Mary's value as an interpreter and keeper of the peace. He also obtained from Malatchi and other Creek micos of Creek towns a grant of Cumberland, Sapelo and St. Catherine's Islands to Mary, his "sister." This became an important document in Mary's cause, as Malatchi had recently been declared, by a signed agreement, the Creeks' "natural prince" and had rights to speak for all Creeks.

Mary enlisted Horton's replacement, Alexander Heron, to draft papers saying the Bosomworths were loyal to the Crown and that Mary held a special position with the Creeks. All of this activity was being kept secret for the moment. The Bosomworths were waiting for their time to proceed. Thomas, through all this paperwork, was not only arguing for Mary's claims, he was now developing an argument for the Creeks being treated as a sovereign nation as well. Therefore, they had the rights over their land and could enforce those rights as they saw fit. To enhance her argument, Mary assumed her Native American name Coosapankesa, meaning "language bearer."

In 1749, Mary, Thomas, the Creek representatives and trader friends descended on Savannah. It was the equivalent of a civil riot, with all parties seeking to have their rights upheld. Abraham, Thomas's brother, had been in England on behalf of Mary and Thomas. He secured some presents for the Native Americans and the Bosomworths. With this encouragement, Malatchi and other Indians headed to Savannah.

What awaited them was Georgia governor William Stephens. He did not like Mary and was determined not to let her have any of the supplies and put the Bosomworths in their place. The Bosomworths and Creeks, as was custom, met at a predetermined place (Cowpens) outside of Savanah and were to be escorted by some militiamen into Savannah. One of the first things the magistrates did was to choose John Dennard as translator. Next, Thomas, in full priest regalia, and Mary by his side, led the Indians into Savannah behind the militia. This was interpreted as an act of treason. When they arrived, Malatchi asked if Mary was to be jailed and that was why she was not to be the translator. The magistrate said no.

But at the presentation of Mary's claims, the officials addressed Thomas and not Mary. They asked if she was Christian and had she been baptized. They queried Thomas had she had the sacrament, had she stood as godmother and so forth. The intent was to question her Christianity and therefore prove she was not English. Then, in a final attempt to trick Thomas by a conundrum, they asked whether she was Creek or British. They were attempting to deny Mary's claim based on her not being British, and if she wanted her claims satisfied, she would have to deny her Creek self in front of her Creek family. Mary told them she was the queen of the Creeks, and she and Malatchi left the meeting in protest. But some of the other Creeks stayed behind, probably not wanting to risk losing the expected gifts.

That evening, Malatchi and others proceeded angrily throughout Savannah, beating a drum to show disapproval of how things were going. Having a mico

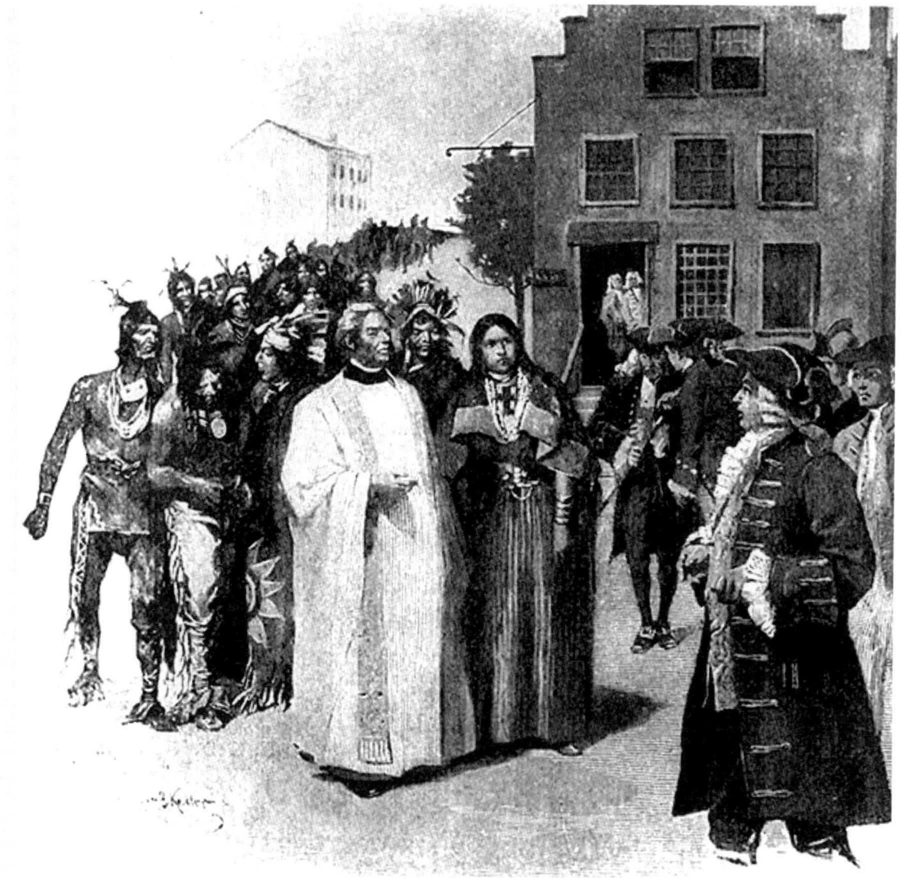

Mary and Thomas Bosomworth leading Creeks into Savannah. First Lessons in Georgia History (1922), *by Lawton Evans.*

beating a war drum and marching through the streets of Savannah did not sit well with the governor and magistrates. They arrested Adam Bosomworth and other colonists who participated. They took Malatchi back to the governor's house, and despite rumors that the governor had been beheaded by the Indians, he was able to meet with them, with his head fully attached. Mary, angered at the arrests of her friends, stormed into this meeting and pronounced that she was tired of the white people's ways, cursed Oglethorpe and denied her citizenship. And then, in a final flourish, she stamped her foot and declared the very ground they stood on was hers. This, of course, was referring to when she had given up the Yamacraw Bluff for Oglethorpe to build Savannah. The governor had her arrested at this point.

After everyone cooled down, they released Mary and Adam on the condition the Creeks would meet with the colonists in the morning. They agreed and went to their camp outside of Savannah for the night. But the two sides were unable to meet until three o'clock the next day, because the Creeks had drank all night and could not make it in the morning. At this meeting, Governor Stephens decided to use the divide and conquer tactic. He asked Malatchi if he knew the Bosomworths wanted all the presents for themselves. This caught the Creeks by surprise. They were not aware that the Bosomoworths wanted any of the gifts. He furthermore asked, as if he was confused, who was the chief, Mary or Malatchi? This infuriated Malatchi, who replied he could never be under an old woman. Malatchi disavowed Mary's claims. The governor had what he wanted, ended the meeting and suggested they go to a tavern to celebrate. Mary heard what had transpired. No one can imagine what this felt like. The British not only denied her claims, but they often belittled her and diminished the sacrifices she had made for them. Malatchi, her kin, had acted as her Judas, denying her position with the Creeks. While her title may not have been queen, because the Creeks did not have such a title, she was considered "a beloved woman," the highest honor for women in the matrilineal Creek society. While the Bosomworths wanted some of the goods, it was after all the work of Mary, Thomas and Abraham (who had done the groundwork in England) that had made the gifts possible. So to say she was out of control when she entered the tavern would be an understatement. It was as though all the years of working within the good ol' boy system had finally come to a head. She had dealt with the slights of being a half-breed. She had dealt with the British class bias and her life's work being generally dismissed. She was not in the mood to be polite. As we might say in modern terms, she was letting her nasty woman loose. The magistrates had her arrested yet again. These two arrests have been portrayed then and by some historians since as evidence that Mary was a madwoman unable to control her alcohol and language. She was called uncouth, lower class, greedy, manipulative, under the influence of her husband, alcoholic and quick-tempered. To the best of our knowledge, Mary never acted this strongly and "out of control" before or after the three weeks of this sojourn in Savannah.

The Creeks received all the gifts and left Savannah. Two hours after everything had been concluded, Abraham arrived with a commission from England to distribute the gifts. Mary and Thomas, who were empty-handed, were to receive some of the gifts. Instead, they had to deal with debtors and continue their quest for Mary's claims.

The magistrates and governor, sensing an opportunity, began to attack Mary and Thomas and filed petitions accusing the two of treason. They went to the Creeks to offer to buy Mary's land from them. The Creeks backed their beloved woman this time and, after some heated discussion, said no. Mary moved back to Coweta. Thomas was arrested for his debts and later released but with a threat if he did not pay the debts soon he would be in jail again. Thomas and Mary realized that to bring this to a close they needed to travel to England. To have enough money on hand for the trip, they sold Cowpens. They went to Charleston (not Savannah, because of treason charges and Thomas's debtors) to seek a ship going to England.

It was here in Charleston that Mary's fortune changed. The Carolinians needed her ability to work with the Creeks. The governor of South Carolina, James Glen, was in need for someone to act as a Creek agent. The Creeks and Cherokees had been at war ever since the Yamasee War. While the Creeks signed peace treaties with the Carolinians, they had not stopped their war with the Cherokees. They were upset that the Cherokees had sided with the Carolinians in the war. In fact, some say that the turning part of the war was when the Cherokees joined forces with the Carolinians. But the Cherokees had invited several Creek leaders to a white flag meeting to discuss peace. Nothing came of the meeting, but afterward, the Cherokees had slain all of the Creek leaders despite the peaceable nature of the meeting. So the bad blood that existed between the two was over thirty years old.

The task laid before any Creek agent was enormous. A Creek Indian had killed six to ten Cherokees in the Charleston city limits while under the protection of the governor. Many believed it was Acorn Whistler and his followers. Normally, if an Indian killed a white man, the government would ask the tribe of the Indian who had committed the crime to execute the murderer. But here, for the first time, they were asking for an execution of an Indian for killing another Indian. Plus, the Creeks took a Cherokee prisoner and stole supplies. The Charlestonians were asking that the prisoner be released and the stolen goods be given back. The Creeks were in no mood to do this. The Coweta Creeks, ever since the Savannah fiasco, had been causing disturbances because they were tired of being used by the English. So the chore was almost impossible. But Governor Glen was convinced if anyone could succeed, it was Mary. After a couple weeks of haggling over her price, Mary signed an agreement with the South Carolina government. Of course, the underlying threat was that if the Creeks did not give satisfaction, the colonists' army would have to come and forcefully make the Creeks comply. For Mary, it was not the businesswoman alone who accepted the work but the beloved woman who cared for her talwa.

Mary met with Malatchi and other leaders of Coweta. She explained the demands and worked diligently with them as they thought through their choices. It was there in Malatchi's lodge that the Creeks saw the quality of the beloved woman at her best. Mary framed the issue not as one imposed from outside but as an internal affair that they needed to address. Their relationship with South Carolina was at stake, and they needed to determine what they were going to do. She did not push but let the natural course of Creek decision-making (overruling the anxious Thomas on these issues) take place. Several weeks later, Malatchi called a meeting of Creek leaders from all the Creek villages to discuss the matter.

It was at this meeting that Mary made an impassioned plea for the Creeks to accept the demands of the governor. Mary declared her unity with them as a Creek woman. She spoke of how she had many relatives and friends among them. She also told the men they knew what was right to do because even she, a woman, knew. She looked in the eyes of her friend Hiapellichi and demanded that he speak truthfully about what had happened. This put his honor at stake. He confessed he was there but put the responsibility on Acorn Whistler. When Mary sat down, it was obvious what the decision would be. In the following weeks, Acorn Whistler's execution was secretly arranged with his reluctant family; a family was responsible for the execution of an errant member.

Every step of the way, Mary the wise, beloved woman's hand could be seen. The prisoner was returned, Acorn Whistler was executed, the horses and other stolen goods were returned and even a promise of signing a peace treaty with the Cherokees at a later time was agreed upon. Mary's diplomatic skills had won the day.

Now with money and the winds of their recent Creek agency success at their backs, the Bosomworths headed to England. The year was 1754. By this time, Mary was so well known that the London papers announced her arrival. But alas, the board of trustees of Georgia did not see things as the Bosomworths did. Mary's claims for large tracts of land and her status as a princess were seen as pretentious. The trustees had also been informed, assuredly in the worst possible light, of her Savannah incarcerations. They threw the responsibility back on the Georgia authorities. And in reality, they were too far removed to fully understand what was right. The problem lay in the Georgia leadership. This disconnect was amplified by how her request to South Carolina to have John and Mary Musgrove's land of 440 acres be awarded was handled. They did this without much ceremony.

On their return to Savannah, they found that Georgia governor John Reynolds had been replaced by the new governor Henry Ellis. This would be the fourth governor of Georgia to whom they would make an appeal. The new governor, Ellis, did not like Thomas. The Creeks were solidly in Mary's favor now, with Malatchi calling her his sister. The Creeks repudiated any past agreements that did not support Mary's claims. Even John Kennard (the person who had been assigned translator in the Savannah fiasco) supported Mary. The people of Savannah, while they still blanched at the mention of the Bosomworths' names, were tired of the whole rigmarole. And then there was the threat of the Indians; they, too, were tired of Mary's treatment and, as always, offered a potential threat of attack.

In 1759, Governor Ellis, taking all this into account, decided to settle with Mary. He, after some negotiations, awarded St. Catherine's Island and the sum of £2,000 for all the rest of the property. This was similar to a plan that had been proposed in 1740, nineteen years earlier.

Mary, who had literally fed the new colonists when they first arrived in Savannah; who had given the very land for the city of Savannah to be settled; who helped create peace between the Creeks and the British; who recruited soldiers for Oglethorpe's battles with the Spanish; who gave financial aid to the colony's causes; who was a confidante of Oglethorpe, Horton and Heron at Fort Frederica; had finally, after ten years of pleading her case, been rewarded. Mary stood as an Atlas across the vast divide that separated the Creeks and English and would now forever more be known as a beloved woman of the Creeks and a British woman citizen who owned land.

Mary and Thomas retired to St. Catherine's Island, and she lived there until her death in 1765. She was buried on the island in an unmarked grave. Thomas remarried and died on the island in 1782.

11
THE MUSKOGEES, GONE BUT NOT FORGOTTEN

The year 1763 was the year of change for the Creeks. Mary Musgrove died. The French and Indian War had ended, and in the Treaty of Paris, France gave up all its North American holdings. The English were settled to the east, north and south of the Muskogees. To the west was an unsettled land that the colonists were slowly settling. For the first time, the Creeks could no longer pit the Europeans against one another. They had lost one of their major bargaining chips with the English. The English grew in the 1760s to outnumber the Creeks in Georgia.

Thirteen years later, the Revolutionary War began, and the Creeks were determined to stay neutral. But they did business with the British, whose goods continued to be desirable. Their experiences with the colonists were of people constantly homesteading on their land. So when they did take sides, it usually was with the British. But as we know, the colonists won, and the playing field was once again changing under their feet. The British attempted to honor treaties and enforce their treaties with the Creeks from afar, usually to no avail. The colonists—who were always breaking the treaties—now under the Articles of Confederation, did not have a strong enough central government to enforce the treaties if they so desired. Fortunately for the Creeks, George Washington, the first president of the United States, promoted an adaption policy toward the Creeks. The new government was for civilizing the Creeks, and if they adopted the way of the colonists, they would be allowed to stay.

Indian government agents from Washington came to the Creeks with plows and "better" farming techniques. No longer were the men to hunt;

they were to become farmers and ranchers. Most Creek men resisted. The settlers needed more and more land from the Creeks, and at least in the mind of the U.S. government, as farmers, the Creeks no longer needed the vast game reserves for their hunting. Slowly, through treaties and statehood, more and more land left Creek hands. Yet because the Creeks and four other tribes adapted to the American way, they were termed the Five Civilized Tribes along with Choctaws, Chickasaws, Cherokee and Seminoles.

In 1794, Eli Whitney, on the plantation of Nathanael and Catharine Greene, Mulberry Grove, invented the cotton gin, which changed the economy of the South. Because growing cotton depleted the soil after two or three years, farmers were always in need of more land to keep growing cotton. This new demand for land and the worldwide market for cotton made the Creeks' land more and more in demand.

Until 1813, the Creeks were busy adjusting, trying to adapt enough to the new government's ways but maintaining some of their old ways. The Cherokee had a written language, newspapers, a supreme court, congress and all the makings of a smaller United States. The Creeks held on to their old governance styles, continued to hunt and maintained their old "justice" system. But still they lost land and were harshly treated by the whites. America was in the middle of the War of 1812, so some younger Upper Creeks decided to go to war, thinking the distracted U.S. government was vulnerable. It started with a visit from the famous Chief Tecumseh. He went on a campaign in the South to stir up rebellion and start a revival of the old ways. He preached that a united confederacy of all Indians would be able to stop the onward surge of the white men into their lands.

It is said that when Tecumseh came south to plead for a united Indian effort, the Creeks received a sign. Tecumseh's name meant "shooting star," and a sign did appear in the form of a comet in the sky. A group of warriors from the Creeks named the Red Sticks decided to wage war against the white men. They represented but a small fraction of the Creeks and were primarily Upper Creeks. This short war was the first time that the Creeks were so divided, with some Creeks going to war with the white men and the others fighting by the side of the white men (primarily Lower Creeks).

This war would be known the Red Stick War or the Creek Civil War. It was primarily the Upper Creeks against the Lower Creeks. Americans, fearful that southeastern Indians would ally with the British, quickly joined the war against the Red Sticks, turning the civil war into a military campaign designed to destroy Creek power. It lasted from 1813 to 1814. The last significant battle was at Horseshoe Bend. Future president General Andrew

Jackson won, with Creeks by his side. Tecumseh was killed in battle up north in 1813. This would end any large military resistance of the Indians east of the Mississippi River.

After the Battle of Horseshoe Bend, Jackson called Creek leaders to Fort Jackson to hear the terms for peace. The Creeks were weakened, with many headmen killed in battle and others hiding or under arrest. The small contingent of representatives was powerless to resist the terms of the treaty. For the cost of the war, more than twenty million acres of land were ceded to the U.S. government. Jackson's fame at the Battles of Horseshoe Bend and New Orleans and this large land cession from the Creeks propelled him to the presidency.

In a scandalous act, a chief signed away even more Creek territory in the 1821 Treaty of Indian Springs. In May 1824, trying to salvage the Creek Nation, the headmen met to declare a proclamation of where they intended to go in the future. This proclamation was probably written by Cherokees for all to see. The old rivals Cherokees and Creeks were realizing that their struggles were the same; the Creek Nation used educated Cherokees to write and read documents and act as lawyers/agents for the Creeks when dealing with the U.S. government. Leaders of the Creek Nation made a law forbidding further sale of tribal lands, under penalty of death. Excerpts of this declaration are below:

> *On a deep and solemn reflection we have with one voice decided to follow the path of the Cherokees, and on no account whatever will we consent to sell one foot of our land, neither by exchange or otherwise. This talk is not only to last during the lives of the present chiefs but to their descendants after them....*
>
> [W]*e want the talk to be straight, that the land is to remain as it is, in common, as it always has been....*
>
> *We do most earnestly enjoin on our rising generations to be honest and to do harm to no person whatsoever, but to remain in honesty and industry....*
>
> *We are Creeks and we have many great chiefs and great men but, be they ever so great, they must all abide by the laws. We have guns and ropes; and if any of our persons should break these laws, those guns and ropes shall be their end....*
>
> *We appeal to our white brothers to treat us with tenderness and justice.*
> [from *The Road to Disappearance*, p. 88]

Two Georgian politicians, Duncan Campbell and James Meriwether, who were committed to the removal of the Creeks from Georgia, called a meeting at the Scottish-Creek William McIntosh's tavern. McIntosh had been the primary signatory of the cession of land in the 1821 Treaty of Indian Springs. Campbell and Meriwether presented a treaty to the Creeks in which they would give land in Georgia and northern Alabama for land east of the Mississippi. The Creek leaders said no and warned McIntosh of what would happen if he signed the treaty. But because McIntosh was offered a huge sum of money and land elsewhere, he signed—so did some lesser chiefs. The Creeks held council and pronounced a sentence of death on McIntosh. One hundred warriors surrounded his home. Upon finding some white persons, they dismissed them and unceremoniously shot McIntosh and another chief who had signed the treaty. This caused quite a stir in Georgia.

In the end, another treaty offered better arrangements for the Creeks, and they reluctantly signed the new treaty. This would have been the last land the Creeks had in Georgia, but because of a survey area, one last tract of land was left. Within months, this land was ceded too. It had been a century since Oglethorpe landed in Georgia, and for the first time, the Creeks no longer lived there.

Andrew Jackson became president in 1829. He was a strong proponent of westward expansion and Indian removal. In 1832, he signed the Indian Removal Act, a plan that was to move the Native Americans to the far-away and unsettled West. Many of the Creeks who had fought by his side at the Battle of Horseshoe Bend felt betrayed. The Creek National Council finally relented and signed the Treaty of Cusseta, ceding their remaining lands and accepting relocation to the Indian Territory in Oklahoma. In 1836, and again in 1837, the Creeks had their Trail of Tears. They moved en masse to lands beyond the Mississippi River. Many died along the way. Some Creeks stayed behind, joining the Seminoles in Florida or in small hidden enclaves. One such group was the Poarch Band of Muscogee Creek Indians of the Lower Towns, who sided with the United States in the Creek War. They had to give up being members of the Creeks and became United States and Alabama citizens, as a condition of remaining after the Indian Removal Act. They maintained their community and culture while living in Alabama for the last two centuries. They gained recognition as a tribe from the federal government in the twentieth century and have re-established their own government. The group is outside of Atmore, Alabama, on the border of Alabama and the Florida Panhandle. They number about 2,500.

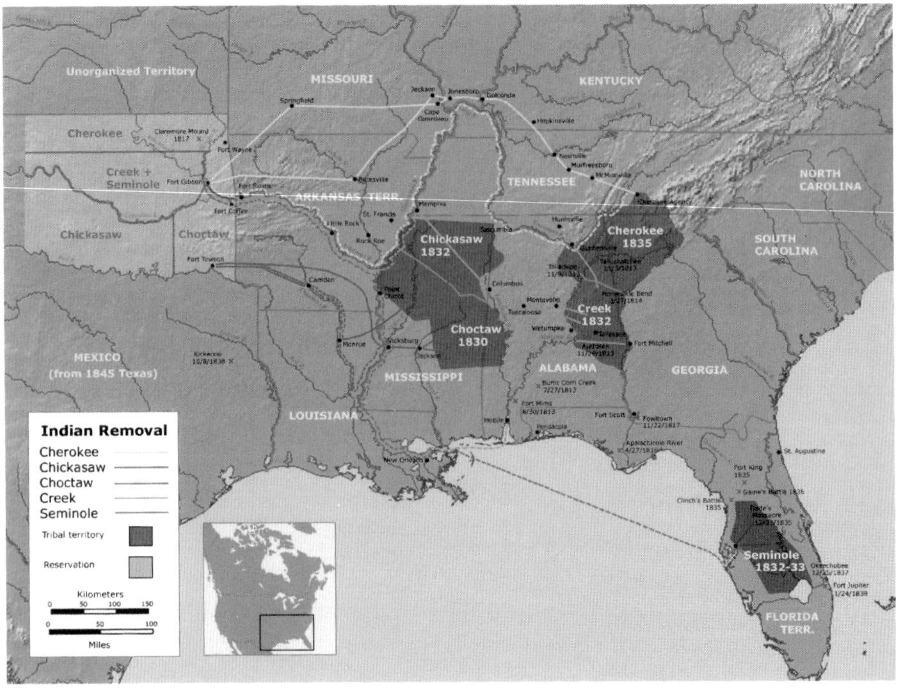

Map of Trail of Tears of different American Indian tribes. *Creative Commons.*

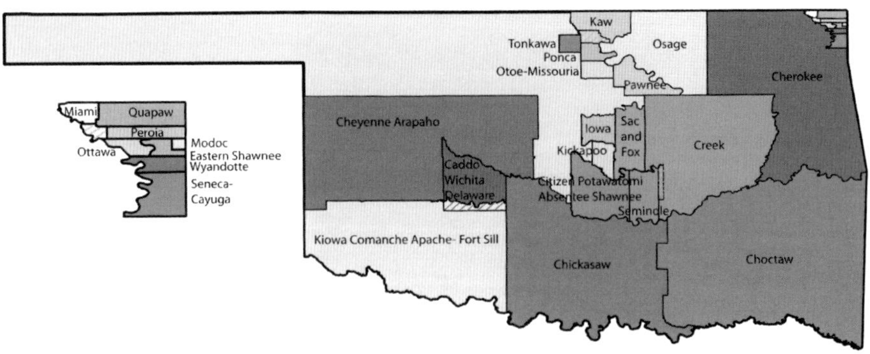

Map with Creek Nation shown. *Crimsonedge34, Creative Commons.*

The Creeks moved to Oklahoma. Of course, the struggle for land and self-governance continued. The white settlers moving west demanded further cessions of land the Creeks had settled in Oklahoma. The government seized three million acres of Creek reservation land in 1865.

In 1867, the Creeks created a government consisting of a principal chief and secondary chief, a judicial branch and a bicameral legislature (House of Warriors and House of Kings). In 1898, this government was dismantled by the United States in the Curtis Act. This was yet another attempt to assimilate them, and as with other assimilation efforts, they lost land. Continued efforts to civilize the Creeks led to their children being forcefully taken from them in the early twentieth century. They were taken to live in schools where they were taught "civilized" behavior and were punished severely for speaking in their native tongues or practicing their native customs.

In the 1970s, after years of resistance, their government was reinstated. The final act was to ratify a new constitution. The preamble of the new constitution reads:

> *Under the guidance of the Almighty God, our Creator, We the People of the Muscogee* [Creek] *Nation, to promote Unity, to establish Justice, and secure to ourselves and our children the blessings of Freedom, to preserve our basic Rights and Heritage, to strengthen and preserve self and local Government in continued relations with the United States of America, do ordain and establish this Constitution for the Muscogee* [Creek] *Nation.*

Today, the Muskogee (Creek) Nation in Okmulgee, Oklahoma, stands as a testimony to the people's commitment to family and their heritage. They still celebrate the Green Corn Festival and speak Muscogee. They have a population of over eighty thousand, making them the fourth-largest tribe in America. In 2004, the Muskogees started their own institution of higher learning, College of the Muskogee Nation. The college has Native American studies and Muskogee language courses alongside classes that train for jobs in the Muskogee Nation. But even today, as a nation within a nation, their struggle continues.

12
THE LEGACY OF THE NATIVE AMERICANS OF SAVANNAH

Tomochichi and Mary Musgrove had as much to do with the survival of the early colonists as any other persons of that period. In fact, since they had begun to settle the area we now know as Savannah well before Oglethorpe and the colonists came, it would not be unreasonable to call them co-founders, if not founders of Georgia. They came not under directives of trustees in England but of the special request of the Carolina government to settle this land. It was the two of them who opened the doors so that the early colonists of Georgia could coexist with the Creeks. Tomochichi helped Oglethorpe in decisions of where to run roads, set the border of Georgia and establish forts to protect the Georgia settlement. Mary Musgrove, for her part, furnished crops, meat and deerskins to help the early colonists not die of starvation and be totally destitute, as some other European attempts to settle America had ended. She also furnished warriors, supplies and money to protect Georgia from the Spanish and other Indians. It should also be mentioned here that Toonahowi was a brave soldier in the battles on St. Simons Island that led to the defeat of the Spaniards and ended their military forays into Georgia. Toonahowi lent himself and other Indians as scouts and warriors in the battle to keep Georgia under British control. Toonahowi was wounded for the British cause at St. Simons Island and later captured on a scouting excursion for Georgia. When an attempt was made to rescue him, he was killed in the melee.

The Creeks set an example of a representative government to the new Georgia colonists. Some say the Creeks and other Indian confederation

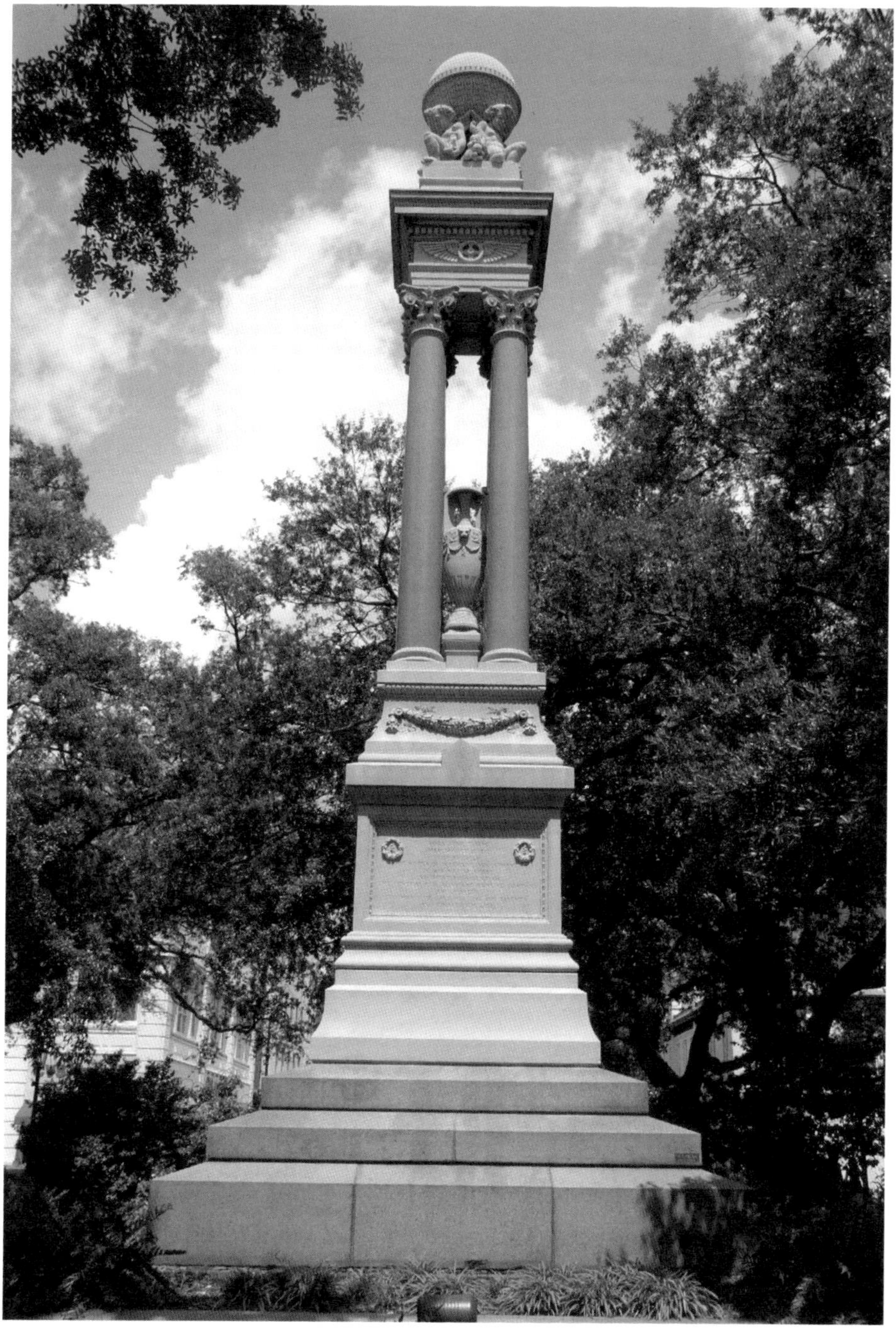

Monument to William Washington Gordon in Wright Square. *Author's collection.*

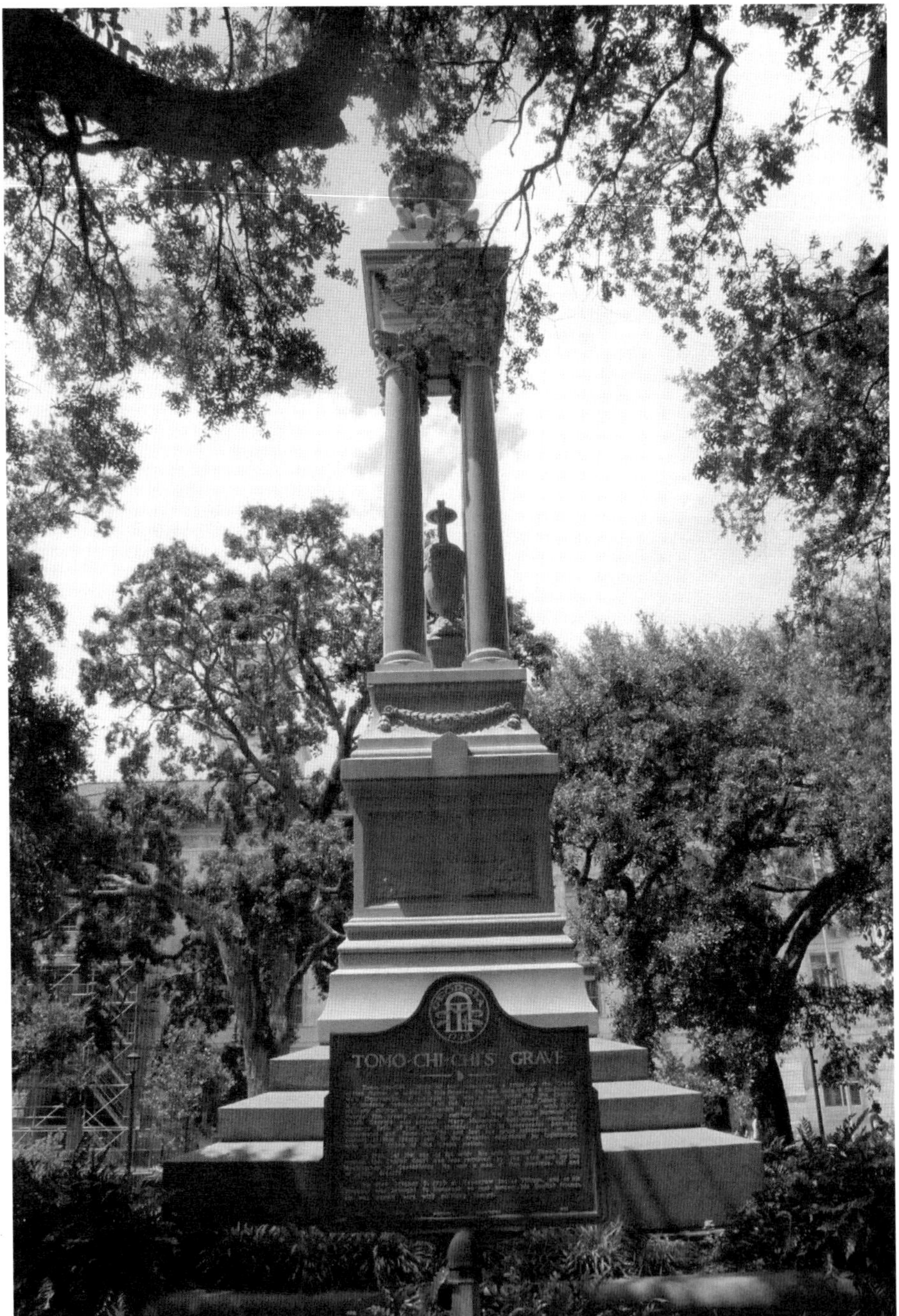

William Washington Gordon monument with historical marker discussing Tomochichi's grave. *Author's collection.*

were, in part, a model for the Articles of Confederation taken up by the new country. Strangely enough, the Creeks were one reason that Georgians so enthusiastically signed the new Constitution of 1787, creating a stronger federal government. The Georgians had become alarmed at the lack of the current government to handle their Indian problem and felt a stronger federal government would have more power to address the issue.

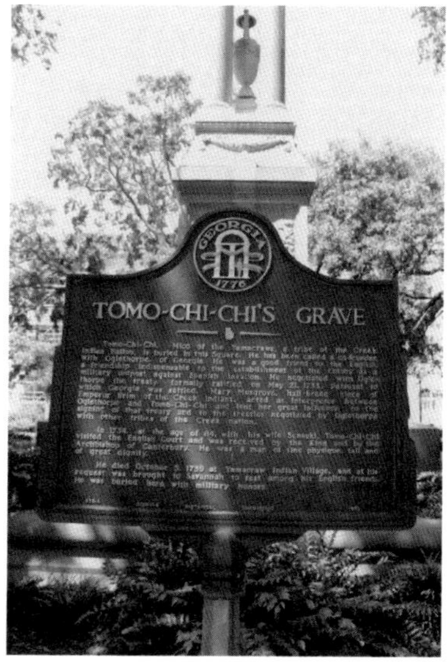

Close-up of marker discussing Tomochichi's grave. *Author's collection.*

Mary Musgrove, in pursuing her land rights, helped change the colony's law to secure greater women's rights. The law stated that if the male landowner did not have a son to inherit the land, the land returned to the colony. Mary, with the Malcontents, helped change this law, giving spouses the right to the land after the male landowner died if they had no son. It also could probably be said that she was willingly or unwillingly a prime reason why the prohibition was lifted in the colony. Because she was so essential to the establishment of Georgia, her trading posts were allowed to serve liquor. This was also one of the concerns her second husband and the Malcontents (who held meetings at her trading posts) took up as one of their issues with the colony's governance.

One can see from this preliminary overview of the Creeks' involvement that they were influential on many levels in establishing the Georgia colony. But these early relationships were forfeited, as the colonists demanded more land and pushed the Indians out of the East. They were eventually pushed as far as Oklahoma, where the descendants of the Creeks live today. Savannah had fewer than four hundred people who identified as Indians in the last census. While some of these may be of Creek heritage, there are no Creek tribes or villages left in Georgia. The closest Creeks would be the Creek Poarch Indian tribe in Atmore, Alabama.

The evidence of Native American presence today in Savannah can be found in historical markers, museums, names of rivers and places and monuments. One such place name is that of Savannah's beach, Tybee Island. *Tybee* was a word meaning "salt," from the Euchee tribe, who lived on Tybee before the Spanish arrived in the sixteenth century. Another of Georgia's barrier islands that bears an Indian reference is Ossabaw Island. Ossabaw is believed to be named after the Guale village Asapo found on the island by the English. Through the years of being translated by the British, the name became Ossabaw. And let us not forget Toonahowi named Cumberland Island after the young duke of Cumberland he met on his trip to England.

There are several museums that document the lives of the Native Americans. The best is the Massie Heritage Center, which dedicates a gallery to Savannah's Indians. Massie Heritage Center is a museum that the Savannah School District runs and was the first public school in Savannah. The other museum, of course, is the Savannah History Museum, which dedicates a small space to the Native Americans of Savannah. Other museums may have passing references to Native Americans but no exhibits.

The historical markers are numerous. There is a marker that designates the former site of Mary Musgrove's trading post. There is a marker in the Yamacraw Village Park, located in the center of the government housing adjacent to the Historic District called Yamacraw Village. This is a park designed by nationally known Savannah artist Jerome Meadows. It is a modern monument made to the Yamacraws' first home in Savannah. This is the land the Yamacraws gave to Oglethorpe and then moved to be close to the Irene Mounds. The monument captures the different peoples who have lived there, including blacks, whites and the Yamacraws.

There are a few monuments. In Madison Square, two cannons and a historical marker sit. They are there to honor the first roads of Georgia. The roads were made by Oglethorpe, who overlaid Indian trails that Tomochichi had shown him. They were important roads, as they connected Savannah to Fort Frederica on St. Simons Island and to Augusta, another fortified stronghold of Oglethorpe.

A monument to Toonahowi is found in front of the board of education on Bull Street. It is a birdbath in his honor with a dedication to the young warrior. It sits there mostly unnoticed today.

The most important monument is found in Wright Square. As discussed earlier, after Tomochichi died, Oglethorpe, with Tomochichi's agreement, had the leader buried in the center of the square. Oglethorpe made a simple pyramid of rocks on top of his grave in his honor. This monument stood there until the railroad men of Savannah wanted to put up a monument to their hero William Washington Gordon, the founder and president of the Savannah Canal and Railroad Company and former mayor of Savannah.

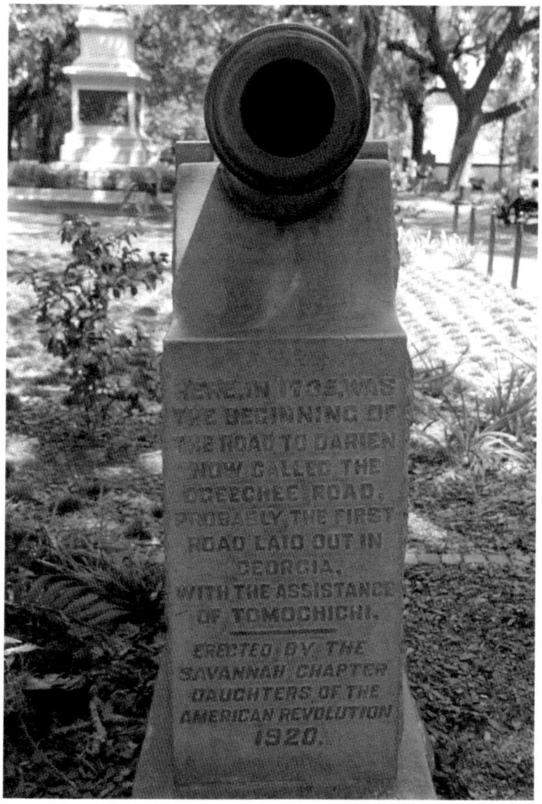

Right: Cannon marker celebrating Georgia's first road laid out with Tomochichi's assistance. *Author's collection.*

Below: Detail of William Washington Gordon monument showing train. *Author's collection.*

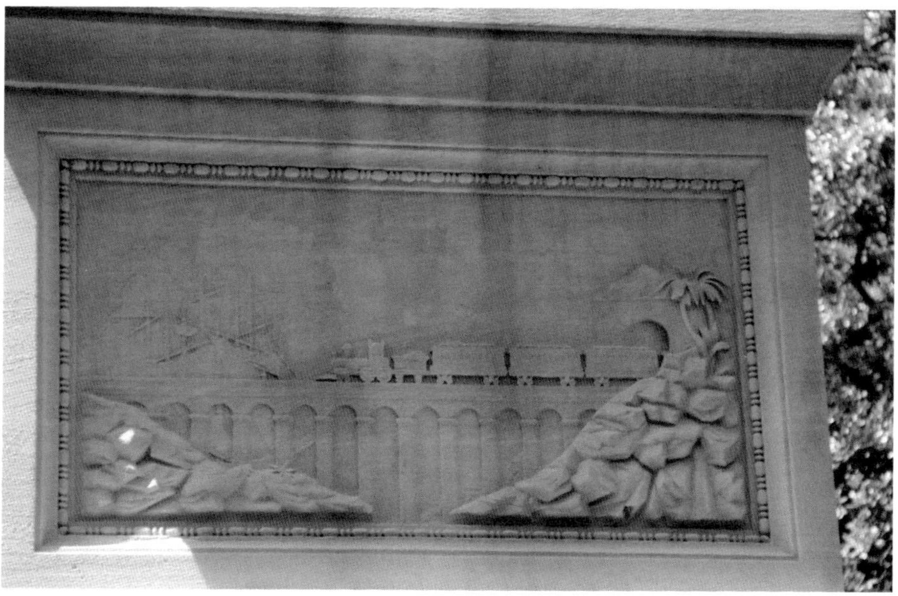

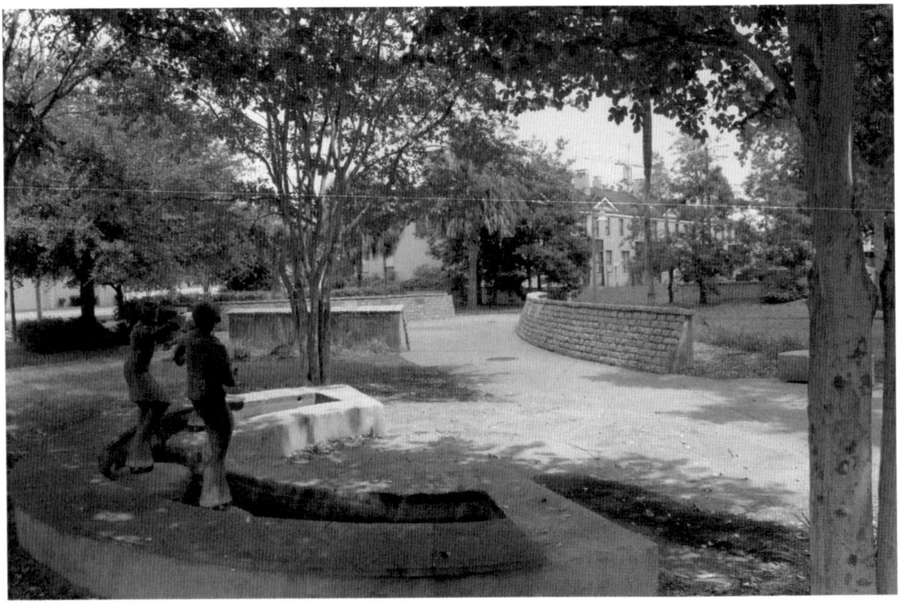

Memorial Park designed by Jerome Meadows in Yamacraw Park. *Author's collection.*

They wanted this particular location because it was on the same Savannah square as the new county courthouse. They were anxious to promote their founder and the prominence of their company by selecting such a spot. So they built a monument to Gordon on top of Tomochichi's grave.

At the time, some misinformation about where Tomochichi was buried was disseminated, that he was buried in a corner of the square. Yet we know that early maps of Savannah depict the monument in the center of the square. Another questionable claim proffered at the time was that the pyramid of stones in the middle of the square was a long abandoned public project. But it was Gordon's distinguished son William Washington Gordon II who said in a *Savannah Morning News* article that he knew the original site of Tomochichi's burial was exactly where his father's monument stood.

A chastened Savannah, under the leadership of Gordon Jr.'s wife, Nellie Kinsey Gordon, the president of the Daughters of the American Revolution, determined to make a tribute to Tomochichi. A new monument—a granite boulder from Stone Mountain in Georgia—was dedicated on April 21, 1899, sixteen years after the erection of the Gordon Monument. It should be recorded that before the dedication service, the dignitaries and others met at the home of Gordon's granddaughter Juliette Gordon Low (the

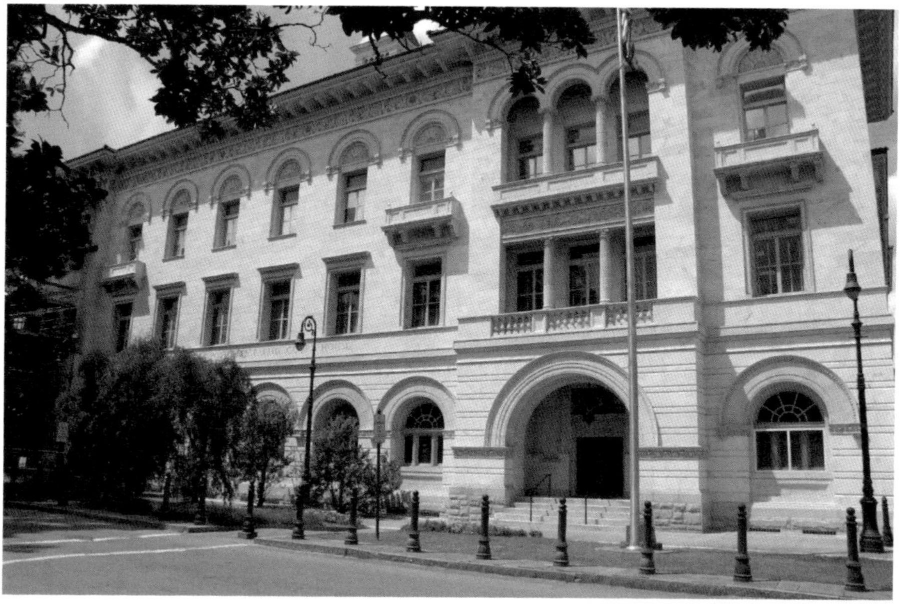

Tomochichi Federal Building on Wright Square, where Tomochichi is buried. *Author's collection.*

founder of the Girl Scouts) before proceeding over to Wright Square for the ceremonies. Today, the new monument is a focal point of many tours.

On the same Savannah square sits a historical marker explaining that Tomochichi's grave is believed to have been in the center of the square. Wright Square is also home to the federal building that once was a post office and today is used by federal attorneys and U.S. marshals. The official name of the building is the Tomochichi Federal Building.

There is no monument to Mary Musgrove, who played such an important part in the settling of Savannah and Georgia. Savannah has only one monument to a woman in a city that has over seventy monuments in its historic district. There are occasional discussions about a monument to her. One such was near the Trade Center across the Savannah River. It was thought the Trade Center would be a great place for a woman whose fame was due in part to her trading post, but in the end, nothing came of this—only a historical marker in Port Wentworth outside of Savannah marking the location of her trading post exists. Also, the Chatham Area Transit has named one of its ferry boats after Mary Musgrove.

We need to reorient our history. The Native American perspective needs to be told. The story must be recorded, not only from the European and

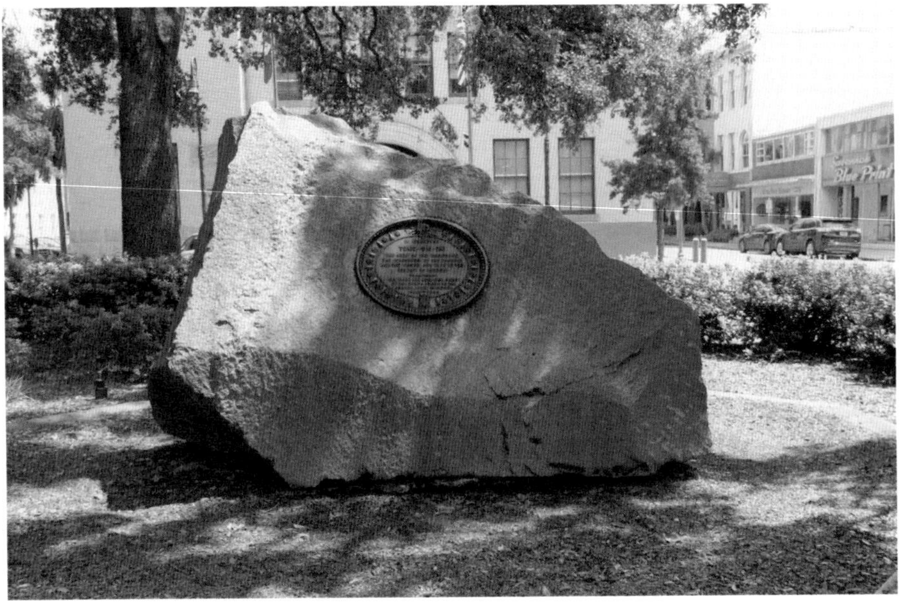

Tomochichi monument. *Author's collection.*

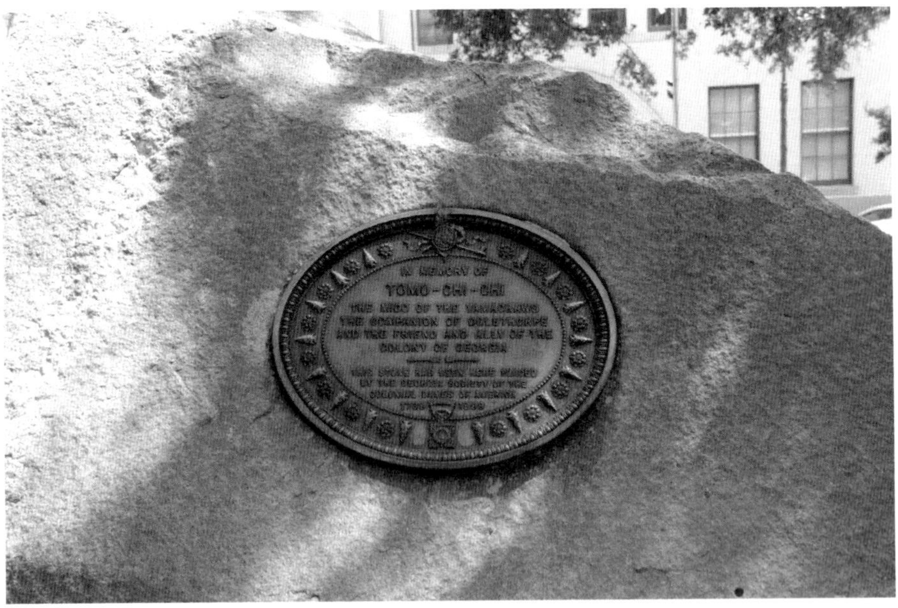

Plaque on Tomochichi monument. *Author's collection.*

colonist point of view. Tomochichi's and Mary Musgrove's stories must be told as much as possible from their own point of view. Savannah currently relates the stories of the Native Americans of Savannah as they impacted the settlers. A more precise account would include the history of the Native Americans and who they were and what they thought. They were, as I hope I have made clear, the agents of their own lives with regards to their impact and influence on the colonists. The beauty of history telling is we always have time to retell the story. Savannah's history and heritage can only be enriched by a true understanding of what could have been with the Native Americans and how we can learn from the past to grow an even better city.

BIBLIOGRAPHY

Journal Articles, Pamphlets and Dissertations

Anderson, J. Randolph. "The Spanish Era in Georgia History." *Georgia Historical Quarterly* 20, no. 3 (September 1936): 210–38.

Cate, Margaret Davis. "Fort Frederica and the Battle of Bloody Marsh." *Georgia Historical Society* 27, no. 2 (June 1943): 111–74.

Charles River Editors. "Native American Tribes: The History and Culture of the Creek (Muscogee)." Milton Keynes, UK: Lightning Source UK Ltd., 2013.

Curtis, Wayne. "When France Tried to Colonize Florida." *American Archaeology* 19, no. 3 (Fall 2015): 32–38.

Fisher, Doris B. "Mary Musgrove: Creek Englishwoman." PhD diss., Emory University, 1990.

Sweet, Julie Anne. "Bearing Feathers of the Eagle: Tomochichi's Trip to England." *Georgia Historical Quarterly* 86, no. 3 (Fall 2002): 339–71.

———. "Senauki: A Forgotten Character in Early Georgia History." *Native South* 3 (2010): 65–88.

———. "Toonahowi: The Maturation of the Next Yamacraw Leader." *Native South* 8 (2015): 89–111.

———. 'Will the Real Tomochichi Please Come Forward?" *American Indian Quarterly* 32, no. 2 (Spring 2008): 141–77.

Witze, Alexandra. "Religion and the Rise of Cahokia." *American Archaeology* 20, no.1 (Spring 2016): 18–25.

Videos

Warrnier, Gary. *Ancient America: Eastern Woodlands*. Camera One Seattle, Seattle, Washington, 2012.

Books

Banks, Sara H. *Tomo-chi-chi: Gentle Warrior*. Savannah, GA: Talking Leaves Press, 1992.

Candler, Allen D., ed. *The Colonial Records of the State of Georgia*. Vol. 4, *Stephens' Journal 1737–1740*. Atlanta, GA: Franklin, 1906.

Corkran, David H. *The Creek Frontier: 1540–1783*. Norman: University of Oklahoma Press, 1967.

Debo, Angie. *The Road to Disappearance: A History of Creek Indians*. Norman: University of Oklahoma Press, Norman, 1941.

Etheridge, Robbie. *Creek Country: The Creek Indians and Their World*. Chapel Hill: University of North Carolina Press, 2003.

Hahn, Steven C. *The Life and Times of Mary Musgrove*. Gainesville: University Press of Florida, 2012.

Inskeep, Steve. *JacksonLand: President Andrew Jackson, Cherokee Chief John Ross and a Great American Land Grab*. New York: Penguin Press, 2015.

Johansen, Bruce E. *Forgotten Founders: How the American Indian Helped Shape Democracy*. Boston: Harvard Common Press, 1982.

McIntosh, William III. *Indians' Revenge: Including a History of the Yemassee Indian War*. Charleton, SC: self-published, 2009.

Milfort, Louis Le Clerc. *Memoirs: Or a Quick Glance at My Various Travels and My Sojourn in the Creek Nation*. Savannah, GA: Beehive Press, 1959.

Piker, Joshua. *Okfuskee: A Creek Indian Town in Colonial America*. Cambridge, MA: Harvard University Press, 2004.

Resendez, Andres. *The Other Slavery: The Uncovered Story of Indian Enslavement in America*. Boston: Houghton Mifflin Harcourt, 2016.

Todd, Helen. *Tomochichi: Indian Friend of the Georgia Colony*. Marietta, GA: Cherokee Publishing Company, 2005.

Wilson, James. *The Earth Shall Weep: A History of Native America*. New York: Grove Press, 1998.

Wright, J. Leitch, Jr. *Creeks and Seminoles: The Destruction and Regeneration of the Muscogulge People*. Lincoln: University of Nebraska Press, 1986.

Museums and Sites

Cahokia Mounds State Historic Site, Collinsville, Illinois
Etowah Indian Mounds State Historical Park, Cartersville, Georgia
Fort King George State Historic Site, Darien, Georgia
Funk Heritage Center History, Reinhardt University, Waleska, Georgia.
Massie Heritage Site, Savannah, Georgia
New Echota State Historic Site, Calhoun, Georgia
Ocmulgee National Park, Macon, Georgia
Wright Square, Savannah, Georgia

INDEX

A

Apalachee 26, 42
Archaic Period 19, 28

B

Battle of Bloody Marsh 70
beloved women 46, 49
Bosomworth, Mary 95
Bosomworth, Thomas 76, 95, 96, 97, 98, 100, 102, 103
Brim 73, 74, 77, 83

C

Cahokia 29, 30, 36, 39
Charleston 40, 43, 44, 51, 56, 60, 76, 84, 86, 87, 88, 96, 101
Cherokee 42, 43, 44, 54, 101, 102, 105, 106
Chigelley 75, 76
chunkey 30, 66
Clovis 19
Coweta 64, 68, 69, 73, 75, 76, 77, 80, 81, 83, 92, 93, 97, 101
Cowpens 76, 88, 89, 90, 91, 93, 94, 96, 98, 101
Creek Confederation 44, 46, 56, 64
Creek Nation 21, 23, 26, 39, 40, 42, 43, 44, 45, 46, 49, 51, 52, 54, 55, 56, 58, 59, 60, 61, 62, 63, 66, 67, 68, 69, 72, 73, 74, 75, 76, 77, 78, 80, 81, 82, 83, 84, 85, 86, 87, 88, 92, 96, 97, 98, 99, 100, 101, 102, 103, 104, 105, 106, 107, 109, 110, 113
Cumberland 24, 69, 72, 96, 97, 114

D

Darien (GA) 58, 59, 63
debatable lands 14, 55
DeSoto, Hernando 28, 32

E

Essabo 74
Etowah Mounds 36

F

Five Civilized Tribes 105
Fort Frederica 63, 92, 94, 95, 96, 103
Fort Mose 70, 94, 95
Fort of King George 63

G

Glen, James 101
Gordon, William Washington 114, 116
Gordon, William Washington, II 116
Green Corn Festival/Ceremony 46, 109
Guale 21, 24, 26, 27, 42, 58, 114

H

Horton, William 96, 97, 103

I

Irene Mounds 32, 33, 36, 39, 63, 88, 114

J

Jackson, Andrew 106, 107

L

Lower Creeks 51, 83

M

Malatchi 73, 74, 75, 76, 77, 80, 81, 83, 97, 98, 100, 101, 103
Malcontents 93, 94, 96, 113
Massie Heritage Center 114
Matthews, Jacob 89, 91, 93, 94
McIntosh, William 107
Mississippian culture 21, 22, 24, 28, 30, 32, 36, 39
Mississippian Period 21, 39
Mound Builders 28
Mount Venture 92, 93, 95, 96
Mulberry Grove Plantation 41, 105
Musgrove, John 60, 69
Musgrove, Mary 55, 67, 75, 76, 78, 81, 83, 85, 86, 87, 88, 89, 90, 91, 92, 93, 94, 95, 96, 97, 98, 99, 100, 101, 102, 103, 104, 110, 113, 114, 117, 119
Muskogee 45, 49, 51, 83, 90, 104, 109

O

Ocmulgee Village 29, 30, 36, 49
Oglethorpe, James 49, 52, 56, 57, 58, 59, 60, 61, 62, 63, 64, 65, 66, 69, 70, 75, 77, 80, 81, 88, 89, 92, 93, 94, 95, 96, 97, 99, 103, 107, 110, 114
Oglethorpe, Lord James 13, 49, 52, 55, 56, 58
Oklahoma 51, 82, 107, 109, 113

P

Paleo-Indians 17, 18, 19
Poarch Band of Muscogee Creek Indians of the Lower Towns 107, 113
Pon Pon 85, 86, 92

R

Red Sticks 105
Reynolds, John 102

S

Salzburgers 60, 91
Senauki 52, 55, 60, 64, 66, 67, 68, 76, 78, 79, 80, 81, 82, 90
St. Augustine 24, 42, 70, 92
St. Catherine's Island 24, 26, 75, 97, 103
Stephens, William 64, 76, 81, 91, 96, 98, 100

T

Tecumseh 105, 106
Tomochichi 13, 26, 33, 36, 39, 52, 54, 55, 56, 57, 58, 59, 60, 61, 62, 63, 64, 65, 66, 67, 68, 69, 72, 75, 76, 77, 78, 80, 81, 87, 88, 89, 90, 91, 92, 94, 110, 114, 116, 117, 119
Toonahowi 52, 58, 59, 63, 64, 65, 66, 67, 68, 69, 70, 72, 79, 81, 89, 92, 94, 110, 114
Trail of Tears 52, 107
trustees 59, 60, 62, 68, 80, 91, 96, 97, 102
Tybee Island 24, 26, 113

U

Upper Creeks 51

V

Verelst, William 61, 80

W

War of Jenkin's Ear 69, 92, 94
Watson, Joseph 89, 90, 95
Wesley, John 63, 69, 75, 80, 90, 91
Westo 26, 27, 42
Woodland Indians 21, 22, 28

Y

Yamacraw 55, 56, 58, 59, 60, 62, 63, 64, 66, 68, 69, 70, 72, 75, 78, 80, 81, 87, 88, 89, 91, 99, 114
Yamasee 26, 42, 43, 52, 86
Yamasee War 26, 40, 43, 54, 58, 66, 73, 83, 86, 101

ABOUT THE AUTHOR

Michael Freeman has lived and worked in Savannah for over twenty-five years. He is the father of three children and the husband of one woman. He has written one other book, *Savannah's Monuments: The Untold Stories*, and writes a weekly blog, Freeman's Rag (freemansrag.com). He is founder and president of the nonprofit Joined In Giving and a docent at the Telfair Museums. Michael holds a BA in history and religion from Samford University and an MDiv from Southern Baptist Theological Seminary. He has been a featured speaker at the Flannery O'Connor Home, Live Oak Public Library, Road's Scholar Programs, Savannah College of Art and Design, Senior Citizens Inc. and other forums. He has been studying the Native Americans of Savannah for over ten years.